Hands-Site Reliability Engineering

Build Capability to Design, Deploy, Monitor, and Sustain Enterprise Software Systems at Scale

Shamayel Mohammed Farooqui
Vishnu Vardhan Chikoti

www.bpbonline.com

FIRST EDITION 2021
Copyright © BPB Publications, India
ISBN: 978-93-91030-322

All Rights Reserved. No part of this publication may be reproduced, distributed or transmitted in any form or by any means or stored in a database or retrieval system, without the prior written permission of the publisher with the exception to the program listings which may be entered, stored and executed in a computer system, but they can not be reproduced by the means of publication, photocopy, recording, or by any electronic and mechanical means.

LIMITS OF LIABILITY AND DISCLAIMER OF WARRANTY

The information contained in this book is true to correct and the best of author's and publisher's knowledge. The author has made every effort to ensure the accuracy of these publications, but publisher cannot be held responsible for any loss or damage arising from any information in this book.

All trademarks referred to in the book are acknowledged as properties of their respective owners but BPB Publications cannot guarantee the accuracy of this information.

Distributors:

BPB PUBLICATIONS
20, Ansari Road, Darya Ganj
New Delhi-110002
Ph: 23254990/23254991

DECCAN AGENCIES
4-3-329, Bank Street,
Hyderabad-500195
Ph: 24756967/24756400

MICRO MEDIA
Shop No. 5, Mahendra Chambers,
150 DN Rd. Next to Capital Cinema,
V.T. (C.S.T.) Station, MUMBAI-400 001
Ph: 22078296/22078297

BPB BOOK CENTRE
376 Old Lajpat Rai Market,
Delhi-110006
Ph: 23861747

To View Complete
BPB Publications Catalogue
Scan the QR Code:

Published by Manish Jain for BPB Publications, 20 Ansari Road, Darya Ganj, New Delhi-110002 and Printed by him at Repro India Ltd, Mumbai

www.bpbonline.com

Foreword

With the customers going digital, businesses have a big need to scale up their technology platforms and to offer the right product at the right time, at the right place, at the right cost, and when the customer wants it. This is very different from how core technology is built in most companies today.

Hence, the modern age CTO/CIO has a challenge at hand, irrespective of the size or nature of the business, which is to modernize IT and rebalance resources invested in running the technology platforms and add new functionalities to the platform to grow the business. That is where DevOps, CI/CD, SRE come in handy to horizontally and vertically scale technology platforms in an agile manner, working closely with the business.

This book treats the concept of 'agile IT' in a simple yet detailed manner dealing with various topics in a comprehensive way. I see this book to be very useful for IT professionals in any role or at any level, especially since the lines between IT software development, IT support, and IT infrastructure have blurred quite a lot owing to SaaS and cloud-based tech architecture.

I have had the privilege to work with the authors when I was at DBS Bank, and with this book, they have demonstrated their expertise on the subject. I wishing them the best with this edition and look forward to many more in this series.

Mohit Kapoor

Dedicated to

All the wonderful folks of the IT industry who are transforming the world one release at a time and making it better everyday.

About the Authors

Shamayel M. Farooqui is a technology leader who specializes in driving digital transformation for organizations and is the author of "Enterprise DevOps Framework - Transforming IT Operations."

He has expertise in driving cloud migrations and implementing IT security, building reliable services, and optimizing IT with automation. He also has a proven track record at building teams of skilled site reliability engineers focused on delivering solutions for optimizing and running hybrid, multi-cloud environments. He thrives on building simple creative solutions to solve complex IT problems and has mastered the art of building reusable automations for driving efficiency in IT/business processes and cloud management. He is passionate about innovation and has developed innovation frameworks that can be adopted by enterprises to drive a culture of innovation in their teams.

Shamayel has delivered talks on the adoption of the latest technology in large organizations and has mentored multiple IT engineers to pursue their dreams of evolving into highly skilled individuals contributing towards DevOps, SRE, Security and Cloud initiatives.

He has a master's degree in computer science from Loyola University, Chicago, and a certification from MIT's Sloan Executive Education, titled "Innovation of Products and Services: MIT's Approach to Design Thinking." Shamayel excels as a thought leader who enables an organization to be at the forefront of adopting the latest practices and technology in the information technology space.

Vishnu Vardhan Chikoti has diverse experience in the areas of application and database design and development, Micro-services and Micro-frontends, DevOps, site reliability engineering and Machine Learning.

With an ability to conduct deep analysis, strong execution skills, and an innovative mindset, he has successfully led R&D teams to build products that improve the reliability of applications. The products are from the areas of Chaos Engineering, Self-Healing, Launch Control and a variety of dashboards from CI/CD tools and monitoring tools.

He has deep expertise in building high volume transaction processing applications for middle and back office functions at investment banks using a variety of architectures.

He has been part of leadership teams in driving agile transformation and site reliability engineering transformation at large organizations.

He also has repeated experience in setting up new development teams and getting them to a stage of delivering value.

About the Reviewer

Ravindra Prasad Elicherla has two decades of years of experience in the IT industry with expertise in Product Development, Product Engineering, Machine Learning, DevOps and SRE. He is currently working as Technology Director, Product Development in ADP, Hyderabad with main focus on building HR Tech products. He has 21 years of experience in IT. He previously worked as VP, Technology and Operations in DBS bank, leading enterprise DevOps, Cloud adoption, SRE and Agile practices. During his stint in Tesco, Bengaluru as the Head of Software Development, he gained a broad range of expertise in retail related to Loyalty Program, Data Warehousing, Forecasting, Market Place, and buyer and supplier applications and collaboration platforms. His stint at international locations such as Australia, Brazil, UK, and USA has helped him in gaining knowledge of how technology is used in various business contexts. He is passionate about new technologies and has hands-on experience in UI/UX, Cloud Computing, and Machine Learning. He did his MTech in Production Engineering and completed Retail Certification from IIM-B and Tesco. He did a Senior Management Program from IIMC in 2014.

Acknowledgement

We would like to thank BPB Publishers for giving us this opportunity and providing us the necessary support in writing this book.

We would like to thank our family members for the support they have provided us to focus on the book during our personal time.

Preface

In this current fast-paced world, change is the only constant. We are at a stage where people are now able to access high-speed networks over a variety of devices wherever they are by either using direct LAN, WiFi, or mobile data. This has allowed businesses to offer digital services at scale. The technology supporting these businesses is continuously evolving to cater to the changing business model with microservices and micro-frontend architectures, DevOps, cloud infrastructure using multi-region and hybrid cloud approaches, big data, machine learning, and IoT. The COVID-19 pandemic has further accelerated digital transformation of organizations across the world. We are even seeing schools now educating students over video conferencing software.

With this changing landscape, a business can expect to grow to a scale of getting millions of requests in a day. These requests can come from different geographies and during most times of the day. At such a scale, running the applications reliably becomes the need of the hour.

For many businesses now, their success is heavily dependent on the reliability of their digital services which allow them to operate at scale. An unhappy customer can quickly switch to a competitor's offering. Hence, it has become necessary to learn the new techniques and tools that are available to meet the dynamic nature of today's businesses and for running reliable applications.

This book explains how site reliability engineering concepts and practices can be used to build and run highly reliable applications. We are happy that we had the opportunity to write this book at the right time when a number of organizations are moving towards site reliability engineering. This book will help jump start the SRE journey for individuals and organizations alike.

The book starts off by introducing how an IT organization is structured and the basic concepts that will need to be understood by an IT professional. This sets the stage to build on this learning for the readers that are new to the IT industry to understand the basic concepts. The book also works as a refresher for experienced professionals.

The book then introduces the basic to intermediate concepts and practices of DevOps and SRE.

In the second half of the book, we introduce the readers to the advanced concepts and practices of SRE.

All throughout the book, there are relevant examples, sample code, and introduction to some of tools on specific areas of SRE.

There are two key things that will be found across the book. These are as follows:

- An explanation about all SRE-related terms mentioned in the book with the right context for the reader to understand their relevance in SRE.
- Hands-on examples to help the readers understand and implement SRE in the real world.

Over the 12 chapters of this book, you will learn the following:

Chapter 1 introduces readers to the role of IT in an organization, the structure within IT the department, and different teams within them. This chapter also introduces TCP/IP protocol and Domain Name System (DNS).

Chapter 2 introduces DevOps, DevOps principles and practices, and an overview of CI/CD tools.

Chapter 3 introduces site reliability engineering (SRE), the difference between DevOps and SRE, different SRE terms, the responsibilities of SRE teams, and the skill set of site reliability engineers (SREs).

Chapter 4 introduces the concept of toil, scenarios where toil can be eliminated through automation, and hands-on examples.

Chapter 5 introduces release management and hands-on examples of performing blue-green and canary deployments on Kubernetes.

Chapter 6 explains one of the key responsibilities of an SRE team which is incident management. It introduces the concept of blameless postmortems and an explanation of incident lifecycle with a real time example. This chapter also explains the less talked about role of development teams in working with SREs in resolving production incidents.

Chapter 7 provides a detailed explanation of monitoring production systems. It also provides an overview of different categories of monitoring tools with hands-on examples of some of the open-source tools.

Chapter 8 provides a detailed explanation of observability. An overview is provided of the three pillars of observability with hands-on examples of some of the open-source libraries and tools to build observable systems.

Chapter 9 explains about the key SRE KPIs which are SLIs, SLOs, SLIs and error budgets.

Chapter 10 provides a detailed explanation of chaos engineering including the process, game days, and hands-on examples of fault injection; and then it finally introduces some techniques to improve reliability and resiliency.

Chapter 11 describes the advanced concepts of DevSecOps and AIOps. A hands-on example is provided for implementing ChatOps.

Chapter 12 describes the culture of SRE in organizations.

Downloading the code bundle and coloured images:

Please follow the link to download the
Code Bundle and the *Coloured Images* of the book:

https://rebrand.ly/0ed020

Errata

We take immense pride in our work at BPB Publications and follow best practices to ensure the accuracy of our content to provide with an indulging reading experience to our subscribers. Our readers are our mirrors, and we use their inputs to reflect and improve upon human errors, if any, that may have occurred during the publishing processes involved. To let us maintain the quality and help us reach out to any readers who might be having difficulties due to any unforeseen errors, please write to us at :

errata@bpbonline.com

Your support, suggestions and feedbacks are highly appreciated by the BPB Publications' Family.

Did you know that BPB offers eBook versions of every book published, with PDF and ePub files available? You can upgrade to the eBook version at www.bpbonline.com and as a print book customer, you are entitled to a discount on the eBook copy. Get in touch with us at :

business@bpbonline.com for more details.

At **www.bpbonline.com**, you can also read a collection of free technical articles, sign up for a range of free newsletters, and receive exclusive discounts and offers on BPB books and eBooks.

BPB is searching for authors like you

If you're interested in becoming an author for BPB, please visit **www.bpbonline.com** and apply today. We have worked with thousands of developers and tech professionals, just like you, to help them share their insight with the global tech community. You can make a general application, apply for a specific hot topic that we are recruiting an author for, or submit your own idea.

The code bundle for the book is also hosted on GitHub at **https://github.com/bpbpublications/Hands-on-Site-Reliability-Engineering**. In case there's an update to the code, it will be updated on the existing GitHub repository.

We also have other code bundles from our rich catalog of books and videos available at **https://github.com/bpbpublications**. Check them out!

PIRACY

If you come across any illegal copies of our works in any form on the internet, we would be grateful if you would provide us with the location address or website name. Please contact us at :
business@bpbonline.com with a link to the material.

If you are interested in becoming an author

If there is a topic that you have expertise in, and you are interested in either writing or contributing to a book, please visit **www.bpbonline.com**.

REVIEWS

Please leave a review. Once you have read and used this book, why not leave a review on the site that you purchased it from? Potential readers can then see and use your unbiased opinion to make purchase decisions, we at BPB can understand what you think about our products, and our authors can see your feedback on their book. Thank you!

For more information about BPB, please visit **www.bpbonline.com**.

Table of Contents

1. Understanding the World of IT 1
    Structure 2
    Objective 2
    What is the role of IT in an organization? 2
        Hardware availability 3
        Core software services 3
        Compliance and security 3
        Application development and hosting 4
        Enterprise Architecture (EA) 5
        Software delivery 5
    Understanding the IT organization structure 6
    Role of infrastructure teams 7
        Data centers 7
        Virtualization 8
        Containerization 8
        On-premise infrastructure 9
        Cloud infrastructure 9
        Development and deployment platforms 10
    Role of application teams 11
        Cross-functional development teams 11
        DevOps teams 14
        Production support/operations teams 15
    IT security 15
        Change management team 16
    The TCP/IP protocol suite 16
    Domain Name System 18
    Conclusion 20

    Multiple choice questions 20
        Answers 21

2. Introduction to DevOps 23
    Structure 23
    Objective 24
    Introduction to DevOps 24
    DevOps principles and practices 26
        DevOps principles 26
        DevOps practices 27
    Benefits of DevOps 31
    Overview of DevOps tools 32
        Git 32
        Ansible 34
        Jenkins 37
    Conclusion 39
    Multiple choice questions 40
        Answers 40

3. Introduction to SRE 41
    Structure 41
    Objective 42
    DevOps and SRE 42
    Rise of internet companies 43
    SRE overview 44
    SRE terms 44
    SRE team responsibilities 49
    Skill set of SREs 50
    Conclusion 52
    Multiple choice questions 52
        Answers 52

4. Identify and Eliminate Toil 53
Structure 53
Objective 54
Understanding toil 54
    Importance of eliminating toil 55
Process optimization with automation 55
Examples of toil with approaches to automate 56
    Purging and archiving of files 56
    Purging of database tables 59
    Installation/Patching 60
    Monitoring 61
    Checking log files 62
    Identify and Access Management 62
    Vulnerability scans 64
    Infrastructure provisioning/decommissioning 64
    Incident management 65
Conclusion 68
Multiple choice questions 68
    Answers 68

5. Release Management 69
Structure 70
Objective 70
Understanding release management 70
    Release planning 71
    Build package 71
    Test for quality and security 71
    Deployment 72
Release automation with CI/CD 72
    Using IaC for release management 73
Blue-green deployments 74

Canary deployments	81
Conclusion	83
Multiple Choice Questions	84
Answers	*84*

6. Incident Management 85

Structure	85
Objective	86
Understanding an incident management	86
Incident	*86*
Incident lifecycle	*87*
Blameless postmortems	88
Incident example	89
Incident detection/notification	*89*
Incident triage	*90*
Incident communication	*92*
Incident resolution	*93*
Incident retrospective/postmortem	*94*
Incident knowledge base	94
Role of development teams	94
Conclusion	98
Multiple choice questions	99
Answers	*99*

7. IT Monitoring 101

Structure	101
Objective	102
End to end monitoring strategy	102
Infrastructure monitoring	103
Server monitoring	*104*
Network monitoring	*104*
Storage monitoring	*104*

Application monitoring	105
Probes	*106*
Checking logs	*106*
Capturing processing time	*107*
MQ monitoring	*108*
Database monitoring	*108*
End user monitoring	109
DNS monitoring	110
Monitoring Tools	110
Agents	*110*
Transport	*111*
Collectors	*111*
Data transformation	*111*
Storage	*112*
Alerting	*112*
Dashboarding	*112*
Prometheus	*112*
Metricbeat	*115*
Grafana	*119*
ElastAlert	*122*
Conclusion	125
Multiple choice questions	126
Answers	*126*
8. Observability	**127**
Structure	128
Objective	128
Goals of observability	128
Service reliability	*128*
Operational efficiency	*129*
Security and compliance	*129*

Three pillars of observability 130
    Standardized libraries/APIs/SDKs 131
    Standardized trace context 132
    Tracers 132
    Cardinality attributes 132
Open source libraries and tools 132
    Filebeat 133
    Logstash 137
    Fluentd 142
    OpenTelemetry 146
Conclusion 149
Multiple Choice Questions 150
    Answers 150

9. Key SRE KPIs: SLAs, SLOs, SLIs, and Error Budgets 151
Structure 151
Objective 152
Key metrics for SRE 152
Service level indicator (SLI) 153
Service Level Objective (SLO) 155
Service level agreement (SLA) 156
Error budgets 157
    Error budget policy 158
Conclusion 158
Multiple choice questions 159
    Answers 159

10. Chaos Engineering 161
Structure 162
Objective 162
Introducing chaos engineering 163
    Application/service unavailability 163

   Network delays 164
   Network failures 164
   Resource unavailability 165
   Configuration errors 165
   Database failures 165
  Chaos engineering process 166
   Define steady state 166
   Build a hypothesis 166
   Minimize blast radius 167
   Inject the failure condition 167
   Verify hypothesis 167
   Reverse failure condition 167
   Fix any issues 168
   Automate to run continuously 168
  Chaos GameDays 168
  Injecting failures 169
   Killing a process 170
   Network failures 170
   HTTP failures 176
   Injecting multiple failures 178
  Techniques for building resiliency 178
   Single point of failures 178
   Rate limiting/throttling 181
   Circuit breaker 181
   Handle retry storms 182
  Conclusion 182
  Multiple choice questions 183
   Answers 183

11. DevSecOps and AIOps 185
  Structure 186

Objective 186
Understanding DevSecOps 186
    Code scanning for security 187
    Secure releases using Infrastructure as Code 189
Introduction to AIOps 190
Use cases with AIOps 192
    Intelligent alerting 192
    Noise reduction 192
    Automated root cause analysis 192
    Automated remediation 193
    ChatOps 193
ChatOps example with Rasa, Flask, and Telegram 194
Conclusion 199
Multiple choice questions 199
    Answers 200

12. Culture of Site Reliability Engineering 201
Structure 201
Objective 202
Breaking silos in the organization 202
Embracing risk 203
Continuous improvement 203
    Intelligent automation 204
    Shift-left mindset 204
Conclusion 205
Multiple choice questions 205
    Answers 205

Index 207-213

CHAPTER 1
Understanding the World of IT

In today's world, software powered systems and service digitization have reached highly evolved states. Almost every business is a software business or has at least a major segment of its revenue being driven through software and digitization. Have you ever thought about what it takes to build these digital systems and who are the people behind making these digital systems available to us?

Writing code is not the only requirement for providing a software service that can be consumed by its intended users. It is equally important that this code can be packaged and hosted on a stable, efficient, and secure platform which is available for almost 100% of the time. By the way, there is a reason that we say "almost" 100%, and during the course of this book, you will learn why. The people who are responsible for bringing software to its end users are the ones who are known as IT professionals. In this chapter, we will be focusing on this aspect of IT, and understand the roles and responsibilities of IT teams. We will also talk about how security is relevant in these practices.

Structure

In this chapter, we will discuss the following topics:

- What is the role of IT in an organization?
- Understanding the IT organization structure
- Role of infrastructure teams
- Role of application teams
- IT Security
- Change management team
- The TCP/IP protocol suite
- Domain Name System (DNS)

Objective

This chapter will help you in developing a sense of the critical role that the IT function of an organization performs. You will learn about the diversity of the roles within IT and what the focus of each function is.

Apart from ensuring that the software reaches its users, there is another critical role that IT teams perform. This is about providing end user services, which means ensuring that the requirements of all the employees of an organization to function properly are met. These generally cover the client systems (desktops or laptops), phone services, networking services, and a few others. This is not an area of focus in this book and will not be dealt with in depth beyond being mentioned here.

Please note that if you are a working professional who already has an understanding of the IT world, feel free to skip to *Chapter 2*.

What is the role of IT in an organization?

It takes quite a lot of work from the time when a software application is developed to the point it reaches its audience. An IT team has to execute a series of tasks performed by multiple humans and systems, governed by many processes and standards to provide a software service to its users. These tasks are related to some areas that are as follows.

Hardware availability

It refers to end to end lifecycle management of all the hardware that is required to host applications, workloads, and services that are required by the various teams in the organization. This hardware includes the computer systems or servers, storage, networking components, appliances, and communication systems.

In IT, there are typically infrastructure teams who are responsible for the hardware management of the organization. These teams mainly comprise of system and network admins/engineers. A few members of these teams have specialized skills in certain areas like storage, virtualization, firewall, routing, and so on. These teams are also responsible for ensuring that the configuration and design of the hardware architecture is aptly set up for supporting the DR (Disaster Recovery) and HA (High Availability) requirements of the organization.

Core software services

In order to efficiently utilize the hardware, software is needed. Also, software is needed to execute a number of business and operations-related processes like security, virtualization, end user services, HR, finance, and so on. The software life cycle management is IT team's responsibility which includes the licensing, testing, procurement, deployment, patching, and in some cases, troubleshooting any issues that may arise. The software services are managed in partnership between the infrastructure teams, application teams, and the vendor management teams.

Compliance and security

This refers to ensuring the organization is compliant to the industry standards that apply to it and to the standards that the organization has adopted to based on its operating area. For example, banking, healthcare, and the auto industry are critical responsibilities of the IT team.

Also, the IT team is accountable for securing the assets, data, and services of the organization. When it comes to security, all teams in the organization are accountable in some way or the other while the ownership usually lies with a central cyber security function within IT. You will learn more about this in a later segment of this chapter.

Application development and hosting

For an organization to function properly, there are many different applications that are needed. Among others, some of these critical applications are the ERP systems, CRM applications, communication systems, and HR applications. In some cases, these applications are developed internally by the IT teams while in most cases, the external software is procured. The IT teams are responsible for any development, procurement, implementation, and maintenance of these internal serving applications that are required to support the business of the organization.

As an example, let us consider a scenario where an organization is required to maintain an inventory of all the assets that it owns. This is a common requirement in many organizations and the need for such a service could have arisen due to varied reasons which could be compliance-related or operations-related.

In order to deliver a solution for this requirement, the application team within IT may decide to either procure a third-party solution or to build an application internally. In either of these scenarios, multiple hosting environments (production and non-production) are needed to host the end solution, and in case the organization decides to build this application internally, then an application development platform is also needed which enables all the steps of SDLC (software development life cycle). All these tasks are the responsibility of the teams within IT.

Another example of an application is a business application like the trade booking system. Brokerage houses have applications that are used by their customers to book to buy/sell trades. This type of application is usually designed and developed with a user interface, backend services, and databases. While the user interface can be a web application or a mobile application running accesses on a user's device, the required web servers and other services/databases are hosted and maintained by the IT team. Different options to host these servers/services/databases, and so on are provided further in this chapter.

Enterprise Architecture (EA)

Different organizations have different views on the role and responsibility of the EA function. In most cases, the EA is an advisory function that is focused on ensuring the architecture of any new application introduced in the environment is meeting the required standards. The adoption of new technology by means of conducting various POCs (proof of concepts) and evaluations of software and providing reference architectures in the form of templates to the various teams is the core job of this function.

As a part of its IT strategy, an organization may make certain choices with respect to its preferred technology vendors like cloud providers, database engines, software programming languages, and so on. The EA team plays a critical role in this decision by providing guidance on these selections, and is also responsible for ensuring that the adoption of these technologies and frameworks happens across the teams in a proper fashion.

The Enterprise Architecture team assesses an application design on a number of areas before it can be considered as production ready. Some of these areas are security, scalability, elasticity, resiliency, availability, performance, latency, failover, architecture patterns used, databases, and so on. Apart from the ones mentioned above, certain architecture patterns are also considered during the architecture review of a software design. These patterns can be around microservices design, master-slave, client-server, cloud ready, and loose coupling. The EA review is a gate that is established during a software development lifecycle and can be critical to the durability and effectiveness of an application.

Software delivery

The application delivery process usually consists of multiple steps that include building, packaging, testing, deploying, and monitoring an application. From the moment that the software code is written and pushed to the code repository, it becomes the responsibility of the release/operations team that has to deploy it all the way to the production environment by following a series of steps along the way. More details on these steps will be shared during the course of this book.

Understanding the IT organization structure

Understanding the IT organization structure helps in getting a better idea of the division of responsibility between the different teams in IT. As mentioned previously in this chapter, there are many different responsibilities of IT which need the support of the dedicated teams for execution. In an organization, the IT teams are spearheaded by the CIO. The CIO is typically the decision-maker in terms of coming up with the structure of the teams in the IT organization.

Application management, software and hardware management, and implementing security are typically the three core areas around which an IT organization structure is formed. One such example is as follows:

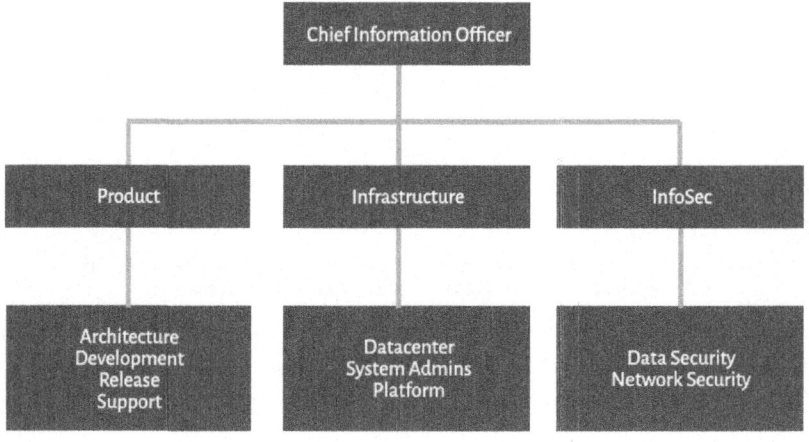

Figure 1.1

Figure 1.1 provides a generic view of how an IT team is usually structured. The hierarchy of the structure may differ with organizations, depending on what works best for them. Also, there are usually a few other teams in addition to the technical teams mentioned such as the **PMO (project management office)**, **VMO (vendor management office)**, and risk management which completes this structure.

Role of infrastructure teams

Infrastructure teams in an organization are responsible for setting up the relevant infrastructure for running various software applications in the organization. They also procure and maintain any vendor software that will be required by the software applications. These software applications can be the business applications that support the business or internal applications for teams like finance and HR. For the purpose of this book, we will focus on the business applications that are used by clients of the organizations and internal business operations.

In the modern world, there are a number of options from which to choose the right infrastructure for the organization. Applications can be run on on-premise virtual machines, **Platform as a Service (PaaS)** platforms or on the infrastructure provided by the cloud providers. It is common for large organizations to have a hybrid model where a few of the applications run on one type of infrastructure and some others on a different type of infrastructure.

To understand the different types of infrastructure, it is important to first understand the three main concepts. These are as follows:

Data centers

Data centers are physical locations/premises where the physical hardware/servers are located. When organizations decide to use their own physical servers to host applications, they set up their own data centers in their premises. This is what the word "on-premise" refers to. These organizations require additional resources to maintain the data center in terms of security, server maintenance, and so on. There are also other challenges like space constraints in case there is a need for more physical servers as the business grows.

To avoid the need to maintain their own data centers, organizations are opting to use the infrastructure from cloud providers like Amazon for their AWS services, Microsoft for their Azure services, or Google for their GCP services these days. In this case, the data centers reside on the cloud provider premises. The responsibility of maintenance and security of the servers resides with the cloud provider.

Virtualization

Virtualization refers to the technology that is used to create virtual machines on top of physical servers. The virtualization technology works by using software called hypervisors. There are two types of hypervisors. The first type of hypervisors run directly on the physical servers and are used to create virtual machines. Operating systems are then installed on the individual virtual machines for further use by the application teams. KVM and VMware ESXi are two examples of this type of hypervisor. These type of hypervisors are used by both organizations that create virtual machines on their own on-premise servers or by cloud infra providers to create virtual machines to be used by their customers.

The second type of hypervisors run on an operating system and are used to run guest operating systems within the same machine. Individual users can use these types of hypervisors to run a different type of operating system on their own personal laptop than the operating system that loads on startup. An example of this type of hypervisor is Oracle VirtualBox. For example, Oracle VirtualBox can be installed on a MacBook Pro and can be used to set up a virtual machine to run Ubuntu. Oracle VirtualBox can be installed for free. It requires additional resources like memory and disk to run the virtual machine and the guest OS. The necessary pre-checks need to be done to ensure that there are enough resources to run the guest OS in addition to the regular OS.

Containerization

After virtualization, the next revolutionary technology is the containerization technology. With containerization, the application code can be bundled along with its configuration files and dependencies into what is called a single "image" and can run within a "container". "Image" is the static version of the application code and its dependencies and "container" is the term used when an image is run. Containerization allows seamless portability of an image from one machine to another and is highly secured as it is isolated from the operating system. Containerization technology has become famous after the emergence of Docker and is being widely used now by various organizations.

Now that you have learned the three main concepts – data centers, virtualization, and containerization, we can look at how these relate to the three types of infrastructures.

On-premise infrastructure

On-premise infrastructure refers to the hardware, including the physical servers within the data center. After physical servers are procured, virtual machines are created using a technology like VMware vSphere. vSphere is a software collection which includes the hypervisor software ESXi. ESXi is a type 1 hypervisor as explained earlier in the chapter. A virtual machine can also be moved from one physical server to another by using another software called vMotion that is part of vSphere.

System administrators will be part of the infrastructure team to create and maintain virtual machines in addition to teams that maintain the physical servers. A simple example of a system administrator's maintenance task is to perform patch updates and install any new software that is required by development teams. The patch updates can be versions released by the operating system installed on the virtual machines, updates to security software, and so on. The software required by development can be open source or vendor software. Examples of software required by development teams are explained later in the section "roles of application team."

Cloud infrastructure

Organizations that do not wish to maintain their own data centers can opt to use infrastructure from a cloud provider like Amazon. Currently, there are hundreds of services offered by Amazon based on different types of needs like virtual machines, databases, storage, and so on. The simplest of all is the **Elastic Compute Cloud (EC2)** instance which is a virtual machine that can be procured from Amazon and is hosted on the Amazon datacenter. Amazon has created its own version of hypervisor to create virtual machines based on KVM hypervisor which is called Nitro.

The flexibility of organizations with this approach is instant availability with a few clicks, availability of different sizes, security, the ability to add more instances as needed, and the ability to return instances when not in use. A number of organizations, right from startups to large organizations, are now using cloud infrastructure for a variety of needs like compute servers, databases, storage, load balancers, and so on. A large number of organizations are currently in the transformation stage to move their applications to run on cloud.

More examples of cloud infrastructure are **Google Cloud Platform** (**GCP**) and **Microsoft Azure**. Some organizations use a hybrid model where their infrastructure is spread across on-premise data centers and on one or more of AWS, GCP, Microsoft Azure, and so on. and such infrastructure setup is called the hybrid cloud.

Development and deployment platforms

Different platforms have been created to simplify the development and deployment process of applications. These platforms are created on top of virtual machines. An example of a deployment platform is **Pivotal Cloud Foundry** (**PCF**), which is used to deploy Spring Boot applications. The PCF platform is installed on a set of virtual machines. When an application has to be deployed on PCF, it can be done with a single command called `cf push` with the source code and PCF takes care of building the application, finding the CPU, the memory and disk resources for running the application, and finally deploys the application on the identified virtual machine. PCF also provides a number of other features that enable canary deployments, auto-remediation, and auto-scaling. A detailed explanation of these advanced features will be provided in further chapters.

Kubernetes is another example of a platform to deploy containerized applications. In order to run Kubernetes at a smaller scale, minikube can be used. "minikube" can be installed on personal laptops to setup a Kubernetes environment.

One more example of an integrated development and deployment platform is **PythonAnywhere**. PythonAnywhere can be used to host web applications built in Python. The specialty of PythonAnywhere is that it provides multiple abilities from a browser - modifying code, mapping the hosted web application to a website address, uploading files, and launching a bash console.

The following diagram is a simple example of an application code that is run inside a Docker container which by itself runs on top of the operating system on a virtual machine. The hypervisor is in-turn used to create the virtual machine.

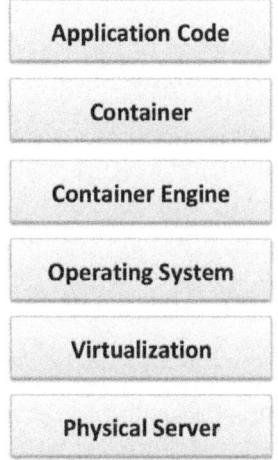

Figure 1.2

Role of application teams

Application teams in an organization are responsible for building and maintaining the software applications used by the organization and its clients. Application teams take the help of infrastructure teams in finding on-premise virtual machines, cloud infra or PaaS platforms hosted on-premise, or cloud to run their applications. This can include the application binaries, databases, web servers, load balancers, and so on.

Application teams consist of different sub-teams within them. These are as follows:

Cross-functional development teams

Development teams use one of the software development processes like Agile, Kanban, Waterfall, and so on. For the purpose of this book, we will look at organizations that have adopted Scrum (a framework based on Agile values and principles). In the Scrum framework, small teams of size 7 +/- 2 are formed and they take care of design, development, and the testing of their software application or a set of modules/micro-services in a larger software application. Given that they take care of multiple functions, they are referred to as cross-functional development teams. Scrum teams complete and deliver incremental changes to the software application in iterations that are called sprints. The most widely-used duration is two weeks per sprint. The incremental change to the software at the end of each sprint is referred to as **Potentially Shippable Product Increments (PSPI)**.

Scrum teams also choose an architecture pattern for their application or a module within the application. For example, traditionally the most common architecture pattern for web applications is the **Model-View-Controller** (known as **MVC**) pattern. In this pattern, there are three main components. These are as follows:

- The model is where the data of the application resides.
- The view is what is presented to users in a web browser or a mobile app.
- The controller is the component that sits between the model and the view. Any changes that happen to the model are updated in the view and any changes done by the users that need to be updated in the model are sent to the model.

The following is a pictorial representation of a flow in the MVC architecture. There can be various flows in the MVC architecture and this is one example where the user request for data is sent to the controller and the controller queries the data from the model.

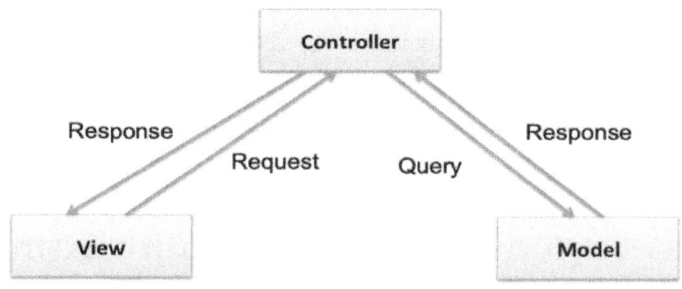

Figure 1.3

If scrum teams build a large application using this architecture, each of the components can become very large and hard to maintain.

Large organizations are now using the micro-services architecture pattern. In the micro-services architecture pattern, the entire application is broken down into smaller services. Each of the micro-services by themselves can be built using a programming language or design pattern suitable for it. This will enable a scrum team to handle all the changes required for a particular service that they own. Different scrum teams can independently work on different services that together form a larger business application for users. For example, there are hundreds of micro-services that are built by development teams inside large ecommerce companies. Once a user logs in, there will be a number of micro-services that will be called to return the content that forms the user home page.

The modern world has advanced to a stage where the front-ends themselves are now micro-frontends. Different components in the page are loaded from different services in this case. For example, header and footer can be loaded from one service, top section from another service, another section from another service, and so on.

A more detailed explanation on the micro-services architecture will be provided in the monitoring and alerting chapter.

Some large organizations also have an enterprise architecture team as explained earlier in the chapter. They set the standards for architecture for Scrum teams to follow.

Scrum teams sometimes also need to use a vendor software that involves licensing cost. With such a need, the typical model in organizations is that the Scrum teams liaise with the procurement team within the infrastructure team.

In medium to large organizations, there is a number of vendor software that are used. For example, Red Hat Linux as the operating system, SQL server or Oracle as a database, Microsoft Office 365, and so on. There are teams within the infrastructure teams to procure and maintain these.

In each sprint, the Scrum teams test the developed code before it is released. There are various types of testing. The scrum team decides on what testing is to be performed and the specific tools for performing the testing. The following are some of the standard types of testing.

Unit testing

During unit testing, the developers test only the part of the code that is newly written or modified. This is confined to a smaller portion of the overall application code. Unit testing can be performed manually or by using automated test cases. For example, Python developers use the unittest package of Python for performing unit testing.

Functional testing

During functional testing, the functionality of an application is tested from a business/user's perspective. Functional testing is performed by providing various inputs to the system and the received output/behavior is validated with the expected output/behavior. Similar to unit testing, functional testing can be performed manually or by using various tools like UFT, Selenium, and so on.

Regression testing

During regression testing, older test cases are executed to ensure that the newly written code did not break the earlier developed functionality of the application. Regression testing includes automated tests developed to test application functionality. These tests are run before every release to validate that the application as a whole is functioning as expected.

Performance and volume testing

During **performance and volume (P&V)** testing, the application performance is measured with higher loads/volume. This testing is done to ensure that the application meets the performance-related requirements which are part of non-functional requirements. For example, one of the tests can be done to measure the number of transactions **processed per second (TPS)**.

DevOps teams

After a Scrum team completes its sprint, the newly modified software or its new components are deployed into the infrastructure that they run on. Traditionally, organizations had separate teams called release teams who were responsible for taking care of this deployment process. It used to be a manual process and there used to be lot of coordination that was required between the two teams to deploy the software.

In the current world, a lot of the processes that were traditionally taken care of by the release team have been automated using the **continuous integration and continuous deployment (CI/CD)** tools. A more detailed explanation on CI/CD tools will be provided in the next chapter. The automations are taken care of by the DevOps teams.

Developed software is deployed in different types of environments. The initial development and testing within the sprint is performed in development environments that are free for development teams to perform any type of change and test. After the sprint completion, the modified software is deployed into a **user acceptance testing (UAT)** environment for testing by users of the software. Once the modified software is tested successfully, it is deployed into a live environment called the production environment. Both internal and external users use the software applications running from this environment. For example, the Amazon mobile app used by those who buy from Amazon use the production instance of the app.

Production support/operations teams

Once an application is deployed into the production environment, it is the responsibility of the production support teams to monitor its health and take care of any issues/outages that arise in the environment. They will be responsible for involving the development or the infrastructure teams where required. They are the primary contact for the applications for business users.

In future chapters, we will see how traditional production teams have transformed into site reliability engineering (SRE) teams and automate a number of tasks that were traditionally done manually.

We will also see how infrastructure teams also use the site reliability engineering concepts to automate the creation and maintenance of infrastructure.

IT security

At any given point, an organization is exposed to multiple threats, both external and internal. IT security is a function of IT which ensures that the organization strategically eliminates these threats which can come in the form of different kinds of attacks including incidents of hacking, malicious intent of rogue employees, or simply carelessness of its employees.

The IT security team has the challenging job of coming up with an overarching cyber security strategy which will secure the assets of the organization like the computers, data, and network. The strategy needs to include standards and policies that should be adopted by the organization.

These standards and policies need to be defined for the following:
- Secured access of critical data and systems which can prevent any data leakage or sabotaging of critical systems which intruders might try to exploit.
- Security incident response plan, which is a protocol that should be followed to minimize the damage from an attack and defines a procedure to bring back any services that were interrupted in a secure and timely manner.

The practices mentioned above are necessary to protect the emails, network, systems, browsers, communication systems, and other services (both internal and external services) of the company. Typically, an organization invests not only on tightening the security of its periphery, but also in upskilling its employees on the security best practices. This helps in reducing the vulnerabilities or risks in the environment that could be introduced due to the ignorance of the employees because of their lack of security awareness.

Change management team

Medium to large organizations typically have a separate team with a primary responsibility to set up the organization level processes, and policies and standards around software releases. Any software that is released needs to adhere to the standards set by this team.

The changes in software can be done to meet an end user's need, improve performance, improve security features, or for an emergency fix to resolve a problem in production, and so on. The processes, policies, and standards set by the change team covers all these cases. These include the type of testing to be conducted and providing the proof of testing, providing proof that the software is secure enough, providing proof that the software change is agreed to by the business or product owner, and so on. The change team validates all the artifacts provided by the development teams before approving a software change request and ensures that the releases are also done in a planned and agreed time window. The level of checks done in an emergency change will be more stringent than a regularly scheduled release of software.

The TCP/IP protocol suite

The Internet uses a protocol suite called the TCP/IP protocol suite to communicate between the different devices connected to the Internet.

TCP stands for **Transmission Control Protocol** and **IP** stands for **Internet Protocol**. The TCP/IP model consists of five layers, with each layer responsible for a specific function. Each layer consists of a different set of protocols that can be used in the layer. The five layers of the TCP/IP model are as follows:

- The physical layer takes care of transmitting bits from one device to another device on a physical network. Ethernet is an example protocol in the physical layer.

- The data link layer takes care of organizing the bit streams of data into a frame. **Point-to-point protocol (PPP)** is an example protocol in this layer.

- The internet layer or the network layer takes care of transmitting packets of data in the form of datagrams from one device to another. These devices may not be adjacent to each other in the network and can include a number of hops in between. The network packets include headers and routers in the network look at the headers in forwarding the packet. IP is an example protocol in this layer. The source and destination of a packet when using IP are identified by an address that is the well-known "IP address." The IP address of a device is different from the physical addresses used by the data link layer.

- The transport layer takes care of delivering the packets to a specific process on the destination device. There are two example protocols in the transport layer. The TCP is connection oriented and ensures reliable communication by making sure that the packets are delivered in sequence and are error-free. The **user datagram protocol (UDP)** is connectionless and is an unreliable one that does not ensure the ordering of the packets. To identify which process a packet has to be delivered by, devices using TCP/IP run processes on port addresses or commonly known as port numbers.

- An application layer is the top layer and the processes running in the application layer send and receive data from the transport layer. Common examples of protocols in the application layer are **Hypertext Transfer Protocol (HTTP)**, **HTTP-Secure (HTTPS)**, **File Transfer Protocol (FTP)**, and so on.

Domain Name System

The **Domain Name System** (**DNS**) plays a key role in the Internet. Its purpose is simply to find the IP address for a domain name. In the previous sections in this chapter, an introduction has been given on a variety of infrastructures to host software applications. Taking a simple example of a web application hosted on a simple virtual machine, each virtual machine will have a designated IP address. This web application can be accessed using the IP address of the virtual machine and the port number where the application is hosted. Considering the protocol of https, the default port number is 443. However, it is hard for people to memorize IP addresses. To avoid this problem of memorizing IP addresses, websites are given domain names such as **www.xfgeek.com** and the domain name system makes it easy for people by mapping the domain names to an IP address.

When a user enters a domain name on the browser, the resolution of the IP address happens in a few steps. These are as follows:

1. The query is initially sent to a first level server called the domain name resolver. A simple example of this is a recursive resolver hosted at an ISP. The domain name resolvers cache the IP address of a domain name for a particular period of time.

2. If the IP address is not found in the cache, the query is sent to a server called the root server. The root server then sends the details of the **top level domain** (**TLD**) server that holds the information of the IP addresses of its top level domain. An example of a top level domain is `.com`. These top level domains are held by registries. An example of this is Verisign for `.com` domains.

3. The query is then sent to the TLD server that provides the IP address for the domain name "fifthdot.com."

Another party called Registrar sells the domain names to organizations or individual owners. An example of a registrar is GoDaddy. In this example, the `xfgeek.com` domain was bought from GoDaddy. After the domain "fifthdot.com" was bought from GoDaddy, an entry was made in GoDaddy to point to where fifthdot.com is hosted. The registrar, GoDaddy, then updates the TLD servers owned by registries about this detail. Registrars pay a fee for the domain name to the registries and it is a part of the fee domain name that buyers pay to registrars.

In the case of xfgeek.com, it is hosted on PythonAnywhere and the relevant details from PythonAnywhere are updated in GoDaddy.

The two steps for setting up the DNS entry for **xfgeek.com** are as follows:

1. The **CNAME** record details that need to be added in the domain settings of the registrar are provided in the **Web** tab after logging into the PythonAnywhere account as shown in the following image:

DNS setup:
How to point your domain at your website.

CNAME: webapp-460533.pythonanywhere.com

Figure 1.4

2. The **CNAME** detail from PythonAnywhere needs to be added as a **CNAME** record in the domain settings for the purchased domain (**xfgeek.com**) in GoDaddy as shown in the following screenshot:

CNAME

Host*	Points to*	TTL*
www	webapp-460533.pythonany	1 Hour

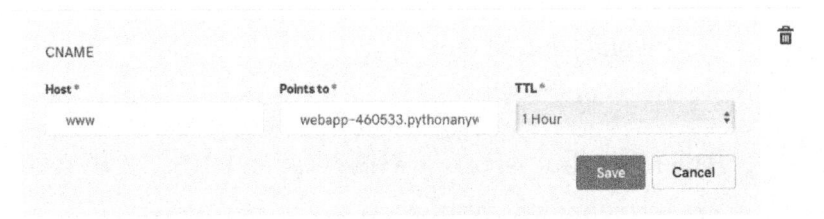

Save   Cancel

Figure 1.5

Observe that the record here does not include the IP address but another sub-domain name of PythonAnywhere. This record here is the CNAME record that is used to link one domain name to another. During DNS resolution of xfgeek.com, a further query is made by the DNS resolver to get the IP address of the sub-domain name. The type of record that maps a domain name or sub-domain name to an IP address is called the **A** record instead of the CNAME record in this example.

TTL (time-to-live) of one hour here is the amount of time that this record is cached at the DNS resolvers; for example, those that are at the ISPs.

Conclusion

In this chapter, we have learnt the role played by the IT department in an organization, the different teams and their roles within the department, some of the important infrastructure concepts for understanding the further chapters, and also, the role played by other organizations like cloud infrastructure providers, registrars, and so on. in supporting these organizations.

In the next chapter, you will be introduced to a key practice used by most modern-day software organizations known as DevOps. The chapter will provide insight about the need for application development and operations teams to work in sync in order to deliver quality software.

Multiple choice questions

1. **The following option is an example of a hypervisor.**
   a) vMotion
   b) ESXi
   c) Pivotal Cloud Foundry
   d) None of the above

2. **The following servers are involved in DNS.**
   a) Domain name resolver
   b) Root server
   c) TLD server
   d) All of the above

3. **Cloud infrastructure providers eliminate the need of the following resources in an organization.**
   a) Resources to develop applications
   b) Resources to test applications
   c) Resources to set up and maintain data centers
   d) Resources to deploy applications

4. The following layer is not a layer mentioned in TCP/IP.
   a) Session layer
   b) Transport layer
   c) Network layer
   d) Data link layer

Answers
1. b
2. d
3. c
4. a

CHAPTER 2
Introduction to DevOps

Since more and more businesses are becoming software-driven, it is critical for organizations to ensure that their software delivery chains remain well-oiled, stay nimble, and are able to scale. This helps them in providing high quality and relevant solutions to meet the ever-evolving and dynamic user requirements. Without the ability to pivot and deliver solutions quickly, the organizations run into the risk of being left behind by their competitors.

Adopting DevOps practices is one of the key steps that determines the success of an organization in its digital transformation journey. Software development processes have evolved a lot in recent times and almost all organizations have moved their SDLC practices from the traditional Waterfall model towards the Agile methodology. DevOps is another step in this evolution as it complements the Agile practices for delivering good quality software services.

Structure

In this chapter, we will discuss the following topics:

- Introduction to DevOps

- DevOps principles and practices
- Benefits of DevOps
- Overview of CI and CD tools
- Achieving balance between agility and system stability

Objective

This chapter will introduce the key principles of DevOps and provide some real-world examples that the reader can relate to for developing a better understanding of DevOps. The key focus areas of DevOps, which are the continuous integration (CI) and continuous delivery (CD), will be explained in this chapter. You will also learn about the main driving factors for organizations to adopt DevOps and the benefits that come out of them. You will also develop an understanding of how DevOps is implemented on different software delivery platforms.

Introduction to DevOps

DevOps is a framework which, at a high level, describes the approach that should be taken by a software organization for improving the delivery of software. There are a number of factors that contribute to building a successful software application. Hence, it is important to understand what a successful application is.

A successful software application can be defined as follows:

- It is able to provide its users the expected functionality.
- It is available to its users whenever they want to use it.
- It meets or surpasses the performance and quality standards expected by its users.
- It is able to evolve quickly with time and provides the relevant features to its users.
- It is able to deliver the expected business returns for the organization.

The most important aspect of the above-listed traits of a successful software application is whether it meets the expectations of its users or not. DevOps has gained popularity because of its promise of defining a framework geared towards providing a solution to the continuous deployment challenge. This is key to keeping users engaged and making them keep on coming back to the application as it meets their expectations on different criteria.

With the adoption of the agile framework, development teams have been able to streamline their development practices. A new release is no longer a huge package of new features which is pushed once every few months. Developers have evolved towards releasing small incremental features frequently. The frequency varies from days to weeks, with many organizations pushing multiple releases in the same day. As you have learned in the previous chapter, a software release is not just about writing code. The code needs to be built as a package and deployed by the deployment or the operations teams.

On one hand, while the developers' focus is on delivering more frequent builds, the operations team is focused on ensuring the stability of the service. A new release translates into a change being introduced in the existing state of the system, and change can introduce instability. Before a new version is deployed, in order to maintain the stability of the service, the operations team performs certain tests and checks, which can slow down the deployment cycle. Unless the operations team is able to keep up with the pace of new builds coming their way, there is a potential bottleneck that is likely to occur between the ready builds and the releases.

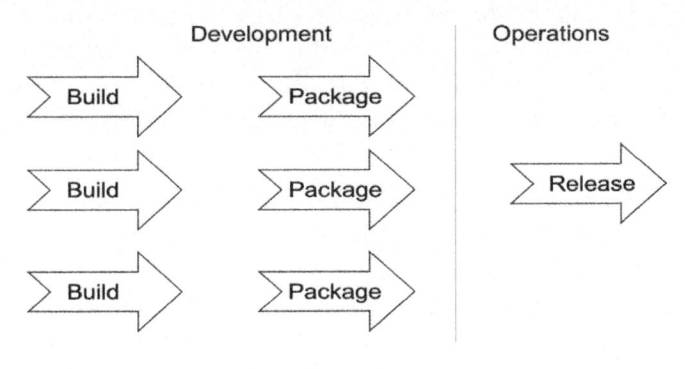

Figure 2.1

In order to solve this inherent conflict between frequent deployments and system stability, DevOps has emerged. DevOps is a framework which defines a set of principles paired with driving a culture change to enable agility in the software deployment process.

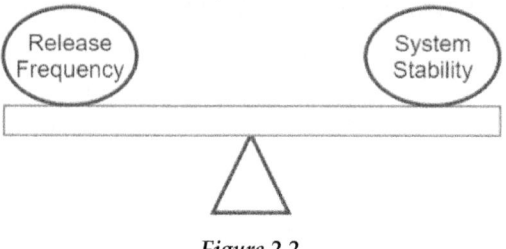

Figure 2.2

DevOps principles and practices

While different organizations will have slightly different variants and level of DevOps practices that they end up adopting, there are certain principles that remain common across all implementations.

DevOps principles

The principles that DevOps preaches are as follows:

- **Collaboration**: DevOps started as a culture of development and operations teams working together; but in the current state, it is the development, testing, operations, and security teams working together. With DevOps, the teams together have a combined responsibility of building software that not only meets the requirements of the customer, but is also secure and every iterative delivery of the software is reliable.

    In the previous chapter, you learned that development teams use the Scrum framework that has been built based on Agile principles and values. The Scrum framework focuses on improving the collaboration between development teams and customers. By combining Scrum and DevOps, organizations will be greatly benefited with collaboration between all groups resulting in higher customer satisfaction.

- **Automation**: Another important aspect of DevOps is the focus on automation. In the current world, there are different tools that enable automation in the area of infrastructure setup, development, testing, release, and operations. Later in this section, we will take a look at the different practices of DevOps and the tools in each of those practices.

- **Continuous improvement**: With the regular feedback loops between development, operations, and customers, the different teams within the organization focus on continuously improving the processes, application software, and automation tools.
    o Frequent delivery of software allows customers to review the new features and provide feedback to the development team. The feedback can also be received by measuring the usage of the software.
    o Any issues in reliability caused by newly released software are fed back by measuring various technical aspects of the software. The technical aspects can be average response time of requests, the availability of the required services, the percentage of successfully processed requests, and so on.
    o A number of new tools are being regularly launched in the industry and new practices are evolving. Development, testing, operations, and security teams continuously research these new practices and tools and implement them in organizations. Certain organizations have separate R&D teams for this research and are introducing them within these organizations at scale.
- **Shift left in security**: With a number of variations that are present in the current world in terms of infrastructure, architectures, development frameworks, and programming languages, the risk of security in software is higher than before. It has become inevitable that security aspects are considered upfront in the design and development. The DevSecOps chapter of the book explains the security aspects in detail.

DevOps practices

The DevOps practices are continuously evolving. Different organizations are continuously innovating and raising the bar with newer practices.

Continuous integration

In the previous chapter, we have learned that development teams consist of multiple developers. In the case of Scrum teams, each team consists of 5 to 9 developers. As different developers work on different features or different pieces of code for the same feature, there are possibilities of issues when all of the code is integrated. To avoid late identification of the issues resulting from integrating the code from all developers, a practice called continuous integration is followed. To achieve continuous integration, development teams use a version control system where they maintain their source code. New versions of the source code files are created whenever changes are made to the files. This allows development teams to track the changes made to the files such as when a change was done and who made the change.

The new version of the software with the newly committed files is built and/or tested multiple times a day. When a programming language like Java is used, there is a need to build the binary (jar file) by using tools like Maven or Gradle. But when an interpreted programming language like Python is used, there may not be a requirement to do a build. A build for programming languages like Python is required only when the software is run inside containers. The new version of the software is uploaded to an artifact repository.

Automated testing

Earlier in this chapter, we learnt that one of the key principles of DevOps is automation and the same is applied to testing as well. There are different types of tests that can be automated such as unit tests, functional tests, regression tests, performance tests, smoke tests, and so on. We have a dedicated chapter in this book for automated testing and we will explain the different types of automated testing and related tools in it.

Continuous deployment

After the new version of the code is uploaded to an artifact repository, the next step is to deploy to the testing environment. On successful testing, the new version is deployed to production. With the "build only once" principle, the software is not built again for each of the environments. The same version that was uploaded to the artifact repository is deployed to the different environments. When continuous deployment is combined with automated functional and non-functional testing practices, there is an early feedback on the new version of the code. This practice of DevOps is in line with the principles of Agile of delivering incremental software continuously and receiving early feedback.

Blue-Green deployment

Blue-green deployment is a practice in which two identical production environments are maintained during the deployment of the new version of the software called "blue" and "green." For example, let's consider the current version of the software to be the blue environment. To deploy the new software, the new software is deployed on an identical green environment. Once the deployment is successful, smoke tests are run on the green environment to validate the new software. Changes are then made to route production traffic to the new environment and the blue environment is kept idle with the previous version of the software. After validating that there are no issues with the production traffic, the blue environment can be removed.

Canary deployment

Canary deployment is a practice that follows the "canary in the coal mine" approach. The "canary in the coal mine" originates from the earlier days when canaries (birds) were carried by miners. Any distress for the canary meant that there were toxic gases in the mine. Miners were evacuated if there were any indications that the toxic gases were at the level of being hazardous to humans. In the software world, canary deployment is a practice where the new version of the software is only deployed for a small set of users or on a small set of servers that are behind a load balancer. Once a certain number of users have used the new software and there is a level of confidence in the new software, the deployment is done on the remaining servers.

Infrastructure as Code

Infrastructure as Code (IaC) is a practice that helps in managing the infrastructure with configuration files. These configuration files are maintained inside a source code repository similar to source code. Before IaC, the earlier approach was for system administrators to provision the infrastructure manually and with some automated scripts in some cases. But this approach is error-prone as organizations scale and creates bottlenecks to automatically scale the infrastructure. The IaC approach eliminates these problems by automating the provisioning of servers and related configuration to create identical copies of servers. These days, Software applications are designed to auto-scale as more traffic is received. Imagine an online store that receives heavy traffic on offer days and a normal amount of traffic on other days. For such applications, IaC makes it easy to provision new servers. Automated deployments are later used to deploy multiple instances of the application. A load balancer is also used in these cases that splits the incoming traffic to the different instances. After the offer days, the newly added servers can be removed.

Immutable infrastructure

Immutable infrastructure is an approach in which once a server is provisioned and configured, it is never modified. If there is a need to change the server configuration, a new server is provisioned with the new configuration. The software applications are then deployed on the new server and the production traffic is routed to the new server. The old server is then decommissioned after confidence is gained in the new server.

Logging and monitoring

Logging is the practice of putting messages in the code that provide different types of information when the code is executed. This information can be about data that is being processed, an error that occurred, the time that it took to execute the code, and so on. The log messages are written to what is called a log file. When a problem occurs with the code, the log messages are checked to analyze the problem. A few years ago, when applications were monolithic in nature, there were not many instances of an application and not many components within an application. So, it was possible for a production support team to login to a server and check what the problem was. Also, monitoring in those cases was about writing a script that would regularly check the log files and send an alert via email if there was a problem. This traditional approach does not work for the way that applications are being built and deployed today. Considering an application is built using micro-services architecture, it will have multiple components within it. The complexity further increases with the variations on how these components are developed and where they are deployed. It is not an easy task to use traditional logging approaches as the different components may be running across different servers and each component can be made to auto-scale. We have dedicated chapters in this book on modern practices for logging and monitoring. We will look at this topic in detail, along with related tools and practical examples in those chapters.

Serverless computing

Serverless computing is a model in which the execution capability or computing power that is required is provided on a need basis. Though the name "serverless" is used as a term, there will still be a server where the execution happens. It's just that in this model, developers who write the code do not need to worry about where the code is executed and how the runtime is provisioned. This is an advanced offering of services provided by cloud infrastructure providers. Serverless architectures help in further reducing the cost of infrastructure.

Secrets management

With infrastructure and application security breaches becoming a major concern, more and more approaches are being evolved to improve the level of security. Secrets management is an approach where passwords, API keys, certificates, and so on. are no longer managed in files but are managed in secret stores or vaults. The secrets are retrieved dynamically when needed. Passwords retrieved from these stores can also be kept an expiry date/time so that a new password is dynamically generated to further tighten the security.

Benefits of DevOps

To summarize, by adopting the principles of DevOps, the benefits that an organization gains are as follows:

- Reduced disruption of services and outages
- Increase in frequency of deployments
- Increase in quality of applications
- Increase in efficiency of development and operations
- Better support for modern applications
- Improved collaboration between teams
- Reduced time to market
- Faster digital transformation
- Better alignment of business applications with customers
- Reduced cost of running business applications

Overview of DevOps tools

In the section "DevOps principles and practices," we learned about the different DevOps practices. In this section, we will take a look at a couple of tools used for those practices.

Git

Git is a distributed version control system. It is created by Linus Torvalds who is the creator of Linux kernel to maintain the code of Linux kernel. The specialty of Git is that every Git repository that is cloned to a user's local machine from the central repository is a full-fledged repository where commits can be done locally. After the code changes are done and committed, the commits are pushed to the remote central repository.

GitHub and GitLab are two examples of service providers to host Git repositories. In the following example, we use a Git repository hosted at GitHub.

In order to clone the repository to local machines, the clone URL needs to be copied. The following image explains the clone URL link for the example repository.

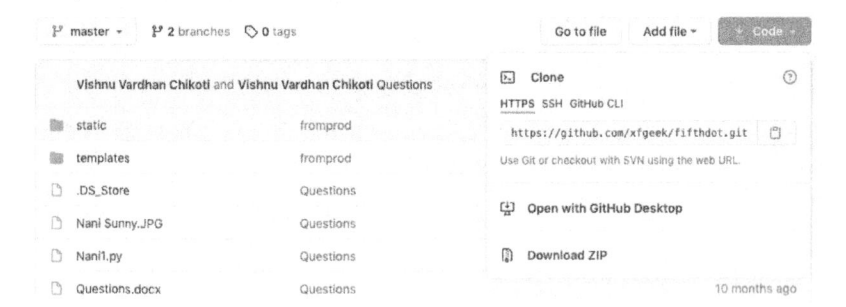

Figure 2.3

The Git commands to commit a change to the remote repository are as follows. This is a sample commit to show how the modified code is committed to the Git repository.

1. Command to clone the URL to local

    If you notice, Git asks for the username and password to connect to the remote repository when it connects for the first time.

```
Mac Terminal$ git clone https://github.com/
SupportPK/fifthdot.git
Cloning into 'fifthdot'...
Username for 'https://github.com': SupportPK
Password for 'https://SupportPK@github.com':
remote: Enumerating objects: 213, done.
remote: Total 213 (delta 0), reused 0 (delta 0),
pack-reused 213
Receiving objects: 100% (213/213), 4.74 MiB | 2.53
MiB/s, done.
Resolving deltas: 100% (47/47), done.
```

2. Command to check the status of changed files

   ```
   Mac Terminal$ git status
   On branch master
   Your branch is up to date with 'origin/master'.

   Changes not staged for commit:
     (use "git add <file>..." to update what will be
   committed)
     (use "git checkout -- <file>..." to discard changes
   in working directory)

           modified:    flask_app.py

   no changes added to commit (use "git add" and/or
   "git commit -a")
   ```

3. Command to add the changes to the commit

   ```
   Mac Terminal$ git add -A
   ```

4. Command to commit the change to the local repository

   ```
   Mac Terminal$ git commit -m "GitHub example commit"
   [master 384f0c0] GitHub example commit
    1 file changed, 1 insertion(+)
   ```

5. Command to push the local changes to remote repository

   ```
   Mac Terminal$ git push
   Counting objects: 3, done.
   Delta compression using up to 4 threads.
   Compressing objects: 100% (3/3), done.
   ```

```
Writing objects: 100% (3/3), 322 bytes | 322.00
KiB/s, done.
Total 3 (delta 2), reused 0 (delta 0)
remote: Resolving deltas: 100% (2/2), completed with
2 local objects.
To https://github.com/SupportPK/fifthdot.git
    4bea2e7..384f0c0  master -> master
```

The pushed changes can be verified in the remote repository.

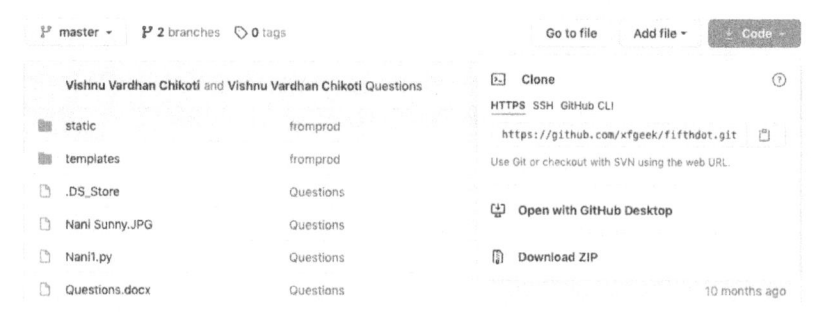

Figure 2.4

Ansible

Ansible is an open-source and agentless configuration management and deployment automation tool. Ansible has three main concepts that are to be understood.

Inventory

In Ansible, the different hosts that are required can be maintained in a simple INI or YAML format. There is an option to divide the inventory into different groups so that a different set of deployment tasks can be done against different types of hosts. A simple INI file for Ansible infrastructure looks as follows:

[all]
firsthostexample.com
secondhostexample.com

[webservers]
firsthostexample.com

[dbservers]

secondhostexample.com

The following is an YAML example.

```
all:
    hosts:
            firsthostexample.com
            secondhostexample.com
    children:
            webservers:
                    hosts:
                            firsthostexample.com
            dbservers:
                    hosts:
                            secondhostexample.com
```

When deployments are done using Ansible, the specific group name from the inventory file can be used.

Modules

Ansible modules are pieces of code that are executed against the selected inventory for the given deployment task. Ansible ships with a number of pre-defined modules to copy files from the source to the destination run shell commands on the destination servers, install software on destination servers, and so on. New modules can be written in Python based on the need.

Playbooks

Playbooks are created to execute regular tasks while using Ansible. Each playbook contains one or more plays. Each play in turn consists of the inventory group on which the play is to be executed on and a set of tasks using Ansible modules that need to be executed on the destination servers.

Ansible works by using SSH connectivity to the destination servers. The following is an example of how to set up password-less connectivity to the PythonAnywhere host.

1. Create public/private key pair.

   ```
   Mac Terminal$ ssh-keygen -t rsa
   Generating public/private rsa key pair.
   Enter file in which to save the key (/Users/vishnu/.ssh/id_rsa):
   Enter passphrase (empty for no passphrase):
   ```

36 ■ Hands-on Site Reliability Engineering

```
Enter same passphrase again:
Your identification has been saved in /Users/vishnu/.
ssh/id_rsa.
Your public key has been saved in /Users/vishnu/.
ssh/id_rsa.pub.
The key fingerprint is:

Mac Terminal$ cd ~/.ssh
```

2. Copy the key to the target server.

```
Mac Terminal$ ssh-copy-id myfd@ssh.pythonanywhere.
com
/usr/bin/ssh-copy-id: INFO: Source of key(s) to be
installed: "/Users/vishnu/.ssh/id_rsa.pub"
/usr/bin/ssh-copy-id: INFO: attempting to log in
with the new key(s), to filter out any that are
already installed
/usr/bin/ssh-copy-id: INFO: 1 key(s) remain to
be installed -- if you are prompted now it is to
install the new keys
<<<<<<:>~ PythonAnywhere SSH. Help @ https://help.
pythonanywhere.com/pages/SSHAccess
myfd@ssh.pythonanywhere.com's password:

Number of key(s) added:        1

Now try logging into the machine, with:   "ssh
'myfd@ssh.pythonanywhere.com'"
and check to make sure that only the key(s) you
wanted were added.

Mac Terminal$ ssh myfd@ssh.pythonanywhere.com
<<<<<<:>~ PythonAnywhere SSH. Help @ https://help.
pythonanywhere.com/pages/SSHAccess
05:24 ~ $
```

The steps to install and run Ansible are as follows:

1. Brew is used to install Ansible on Mac.

    `Mac Terminal$ brew install ansible`

2. Use Python pip to install the Ansible package.

    `Mac Terminal$ pip install ansible`

Introduction to DevOps ■ 37

3. Verify Ansible install by checking the version.
```
Mac Terminal$ ansible --version
ansible 2.9.9
```

4. Set up hosts file with the target server details.
```
Mac Terminal$ cat hosts.yml
[all]
ssh.pythonanywhere.com
```

5. Copy a file to the destination using the copy module on the command line. In order to run regularly across multiple groups and tasks with multiple modules, a playbook needs to be created.
```
Mac Terminal$ ansible all -i hosts.yml -u myfd -m copy -a "src=/tmp/ansible-test/ dest=/tmp"
ssh.pythonanywhere.com | CHANGED => {
    "ansible_facts": {
        "discovered_interpreter_python": "/usr/bin/python"
    },
    "changed": true,
    "checksum": "1d229271928d3f9e2bb0375bd6ce5db6c6d348d9",
    "dest": "/tmp/testfile",
    "gid": 60000,
    "group": "registered_users",
    "md5sum": "09f7e02f1290be211da707a266f153b3",
    "mode": "0664",
    "owner": "myfd",
    "size": 6,
    "src": "/home/myfd/.ansible/tmp/ansible-tmp-1591429426.882112-26069-190844547817392/source",
    "state": "file",
    "uid": 1680393
}
```

Jenkins

Jenkins is an open-source automation tool that is used for continuous integration and continuous deployment. It can be used to automate the entire steps of build, automated testing, scanning software for quality and security, uploading to an artifact repository and deployment. These steps in the CI/CD process can be fully automated and set to run as soon as the different developers merge new code or it can be set to run at regular intervals of the day. There are numerous options in Jenkins providing a number of ways to achieve CI/CD.

The key concepts in Jenkins are as follows:

Jobs

There are two main types of jobs in Jenkins to run the automated CI/CD steps. The first is called the freestyle job and the other is called the pipeline job. An explanation of the two types of jobs is as follows:

- Freestyle jobs can be created from the Jenkins UI and different options can be provided like SCM, build steps like building a project using Maven, and so on. and post-build steps like uploading to a Nexus repository. Different plugins are available for adding in the build and post-build steps. New plugins can also be created as per the specific needs of an organization.

- Pipeline jobs again fall under two categories – declarative pipeline and scripted pipeline. Declarative pipeline is a recent one and uses the pipeline domain-specific language (DSL). Scripted pipeline uses a Groovy-based DSL. Jenkins pipelines are created in a file called Jenkinsfile which is source controlled to a version control system. For example, the Git repository where the source code resides. Jobs are created and run based on the steps in Jenkinsfile.

  The scripted pipeline provides more flexibility than the declarative pipeline by providing an option to use what are called Jenkins shared libraries.

An outline of Jenkinsfile with different stages from build to deploy and the different steps within it is as follows:

```
pipeline {
    agent any
    stages {
        stage('Build') {
            steps {
                // Put maven or gradle or npm or anything else that is required based on the programming language to build
```

```
                }
        stage('Scan') {
            steps {
                // Put steps to scan the built binary or
container image
            }
        }
        stage('test') {
            steps {
                // Put steps to trigger JMeter or Selenium
or any other automated testing tools
            }
        }
        stage('Upload') {
            steps {
                // Put steps to upload the binary or
container image to an artifact repository like Nexus
            }
        }
    }
}
```

Slaves

Jenkins uses a master-slave model where there is a Jenkins master server and slaves are used to execute the automated steps. The master-slave model is used in organizations where there are many development teams and a single master server cannot handle all the jobs from the different teams. Depending on the type of infrastructure of the organization, slaves can be created for applications running on Windows and Linux, and mobile apps can be created and used within the build jobs.

Conclusion

This chapter has given you a good understanding of what DevOps is and why so many organizations are adopting it. The speed and frequency of deployments is very important for software development, and at the same time, stability of services is very critical. By adopting DevOps practices, the operations team can keep in sync with the developers and deliver stable deployments at a faster rate.

The next chapter will help you understand how DevOps and site reliability are related, and understand the overlap in these two practices and the subtle difference between them. Also, the next chapter will provide you an introduction to SRE which will be carried forward in the subsequent chapters.

Multiple choice questions

1. **Which of the following is not a concept in Ansible?**
   a) Inventory
   b) Modules
   c) Playbooks
   d) Pipeline

2. **Which of the following protocols does Ansible use?**
   a) HTTP
   b) HTTPS
   c) SSH
   d) None of the above

3. **Which of the following are types of jobs in Jenkins?**
   a) Freestyle
   b) Scripted pipeline
   c) Declarative pipeline
   d) All of the above

Answers

1. d
2. c
3. d

CHAPTER 3
Introduction to SRE

DevOps has emerged as a framework which defines areas to be focused on for delivering software at a higher velocity and with a better quality. In order to reap the benefits that DevOps promises, the DevOps practices need to be implemented in certain areas of IT. Site Reliability Engineering, more commonly known as SRE as a practice, is implementation-focused and lays out specific approaches that an organization can adopt to improve the reliability of their services and bring IT to the forefront of driving digital transformation for an organization. It provides a well-defined path for technologists to achieve higher levels of efficiencies in IT.

Structure

In this chapter, we will discuss the following topics:
- DevOps and SRE
- Rise of internet and digital companies
- SRE overview
- SRE team responsibilities
- Skill set of SREs

Objective

This chapter will focus on why there is a need for SRE and the overlap and delta between DevOps and SRE. You will develop a basic understanding of what site reliability engineering is and the reason why organizations should seriously consider it to improve building reliability.

DevOps and SRE

In the previous chapter, you learnt the principles of DevOps like collaboration and automation. While DevOps and its practices were evolving across the world, the **site reliability engineering (SRE)** discipline evolved inside Google. Similar to the principles of DevOps, the site reliability engineering discipline insists on automation, collaboration between different teams in the organization, and measuring different metrics (service, release, and so on). However, it is important to note that SRE is a more specific way of doing DevOps, similar to how extreme programming is a more specific implementation of Agile. The engineers working in SRE teams are called the site reliability engineers.

The core principles of DevOps that are defined in the previous chapters are collaboration, automation, continuous improvement, and shift-left in security. SRE takes these principles defined by DevOps and puts them into practice in the following manner.

- SRE enables collaboration between teams by creating common goals between development and operations teams such as improving the availability of systems or meeting the **SLO (service level objective)** which you will be learning about in the coming chapters. Also, SRE promotes the Infrastructure as Code or IAC practice which requires the two teams to work in a partnership model.
- SLOs are setups based on **SLAs (service-level agreements)** that are related to agreements on availability, response time, and so on. SLAs are actual agreements with end customers and may include fines if they are not met.
- Automation is a key principle in DevOps, and SRE puts this principle into practice by focusing on using the power of automation to eliminate toil in the infrastructure and deployment teams world. A site reliability engineer in an

organization is required to identify the manual work or toil in the operations teams and automate those tasks.
- The scope of continuous improvement identified as another DevOps principle is very vast. This is implemented in many ways within SRE practice. Once the availability target of a service (knows as SLO) is decided, improvement in the different areas which contribute to the availability (known as SLIs) are put into place. In many cases, these improvements are implemented in several iterations and it can be a cyclic process with the service evolving with time.
- The shift left in security is achieved within SRE by first embedding security practices upfront in the various processes often achieved by means of DevSecOps, and then automating a number of these security practices to enable shift left.

A few terms which were mentioned in the above explanations will be dealt with in detail in the later section of this chapter.

Rise of internet companies

If we look at the evolution of DevOps and SRE, it is to be noticed that both have a lot of focus on automation right from the build, deploy, and operate areas. If we take a step back and look at why there was a need for this, the simple answer is that these have evolved based on a need from rapidly growing internet companies. Internet companies are the companies that provide services over the internet and have millions of users using their services. These may be social media companies, ecommerce companies, ride sharing companies, payment companies, and so on. With the number of users and the scale at which these companies operate, it is impossible to maintain all their systems and services manually. It is also not possible to manually increase the infrastructure and number of services based on a growing user demand. For example, during festival or offer days, there will be high load on the ecommerce applications. The services of these applications will need to be temporarily scaled up and scaled down after the sale period ends. This scaling up and scaling down will be seamless or can happen with minimal effort if automation is in place, right from the infrastructure setup to deploying, and then finally operating the service.

A number of tools and services in the areas of continuous integration, continuous delivery, infrastructure automation, load balancers, secret vaults, logging, monitoring, and so on. have evolved out of this need to reliably operate at scale. Given the number of users of these companies and the competition they have with other companies in the same segment, it is important to run the services reliably. If there are any issues in any of the services, they need to be fixed really quickly to reduce the revenue and reputational impact.

Different internet companies have used their own ways to automate tasks in production and to operate at scale. Some of these companies have also open sourced their internal tools that were built to meet these purposes. For example, Google has open sourced Kubernetes, Netflix has recently open sourced its incident management tool called Dispatch and Alibaba has open sourced its chaos experimentation solution called ChaosBlade.

SRE overview

SRE as a term was coined by Ben Treynor Sloss at Google. In the first book that Google released on SRE, the introduction chapter explains SRE as follows:

SRE is what happens when you ask a software engineer to design an operations team.

This one line explains why there is so much focus on automation by SREs by eliminating manual tasks and how well they can coordinate with development teams in helping them design systems that can be operated reliably. When needed, SRE teams also have the ability to design and implement a new solution to manage the runtime of services and run them reliably.

After the inception of SRE in Google, there are many companies that have now adopted the SRE practices. Some of these companies have done their own tweaks to processes and terminology for their SRE transformation.

SRE terms

There are some specific terms and concepts in SRE that will be covered in great detail in the future chapters. The following section gives a short explanation of the specific key terms that need to be understood to become a site reliability engineer.

Further in the book, "SRE" will refer to site reliability engineering and "SREs" will refer to site reliability engineers.

Toil

Toil is defined as any work done by an operations team member that is currently manual, repeatedly performed, and can be automated. By automating these tasks and eliminating toil, the SREs can focus on tasks that will add more value to the organization. It is recommended that SREs spend at least 50% of their time on automations and engineering work.

Eliminating toil also results in dollar savings since lesser number of resources are required in SRE teams. In a later chapter, we will take a look at different types of tasks that can be automated.

Service level indicator (SLI)

Service level indicator (SLI) is a measure of how a service is performing at a given point in time. The performance can be in terms of service availability, number of requests within acceptable response time, number of failed requests, quality of data in responses, and so on.

Service level objective (SLO)

Service level objective (SLO) is the target for the service level. For example, an availability target of 99.9%, successful transactions rate of 99%, and so on. SLOs are agreed with the business and SREs ensure that the SLI is better than SLO. It is to be noted that the higher the number of 9's in the SLO, the more difficult and more costlier it is to achieve the target SLO. SLOs should be set up with a reasonable target based on the usage of the service. For example, an online banking application used by the bank's customers is expected to be available 24*7 when compared to an internal banking application used only by the bank staff.

There are a number of techniques/approaches used by development teams and SREs to meet the SLOs. These include running multiple instances of services behind a load balancer to achieve high availability and also to balance the load between the multiple instances, automatically spinning up new instances when there is a higher load than expected, caching at different layers to speed up responses, using **content delivery networks (CDNs)** for static content, setting up Geo DNS for routing user requests to the nearest server location, and so on. All of these techniques will be explained in detail in the future chapters.

Error budget

Error budget as the name suggests is the budget that can be used up for errors. Now, it is important to look at why we need a budget for errors. Errors are actually not a good thing but why do SRE teams maintain budget for errors. The answer to this is that SREs accept failure as normal. There are numerous known approaches that can be applied to avoid errors—right from architecture, coding, testing, monitoring, and so on. However, there can still be some errors/ failures due to reasons not in control of an organization or due to other unforeseen circumstances or merely bugs that still escape different types of testing and reach production. Example of issues that are not in control of SREs are network issues when users are in low bandwidth areas.

Error budget is calculated using a formula and is tracked every week, two weeks, or a different duration as per the organization's need. When the SLO is set against availability, the error budget is calculated as the amount of time that the service can remain unavailable to the users. And when the SLO is against the responses from the service, the error budget is the number of responses that cannot meet the service level standard stated in the SLO.

For example, if the availability of the SLO is 99.9%, the service can be down for about 525 minutes based on the following calculation:

(0.1 * 365 * 24 * 60) / 100 = 525.6

Another example of SLO can be on the number of responses with errors. With a billion requests per year and an SLO of 99.9%, the number of responses with errors can be 1 million across the entire year.

SREs also maintain an error budget policy that states what needs to be done when the error budget is exhausted. For example, if the service regularly goes down due to issues in software code and the error budget related to availability is exhausted, SREs can stop the code releases for that service until the underlying problem is resolved.

Blameless Postmortems

Another impact of SRE is that the incident retrospectives are conducted with a "blameless" mindset. If you are an experienced engineer, you can recollect instances where your service had a major outage in production and the post incident review calls tended to blame on the team as the cause of the outage. SREs, on the other hand, focus on the problem and fix it to avoid the same problem in the future than blaming the team or individual or a vendor for the outage.

Launch checklist

Before launching new products or services, SREs maintain a launch checklist to ensure that the reliability requirements for the new services are met. Organizations maintain a separate team within the SRE organization that maintains the launch checklist for the organization. SRE teams ideally automate verification of the launch checklist or automate getting relevant data for verifying the launch checklist. This is in line with the target to have maximum automation and minimum toil.

Mean time to detect (MTTD), Mean time to recover (MTTR), and mean time between failures (MTBF)

Mean time to detect (MTTD) is the average amount of time to identify that there is an outage or an issue in the production service.

Mean time to recover (or repair/resolve/restore), also known as, MTTR is the average amount of time it takes to restore a service from an outage by fixing the underlying issue.

As an example, consider that there were five issues in a particular month for an application with below the time that was taken to detect and recover. In this example, the MTTD for the month is 14 minutes and MTTR is 26 minutes.

Issue Number	Time to detect (mins)	Time to recover (mins)
1	5	30
2	20	10
3	15	60
4	10	20
5	20	10

Table 3.1

Mean time between failures (MTBF) is the average amount of time between two failures in the production service. A well-designed system that is designed and tested for reliability will have higher MTBF.

Let's take the above example and add a column that shows what the time was between the earlier failure and the current failure in days. In this example, MTBF is 5 days.

Issue Number	Time to detect (mins)	Time to recover (mins)	Time from previous failure (days)
1	5	30	2
2	20	10	5
3	15	60	6
4	10	20	2
5	20	10	10

Table 3.2

There are two main cases where it is critical to restore a service quickly. These are as follows:

- When there are a large number of users.
- When the user base is low but they perform high value transactions.

In the previous section, we learnt about the internet companies that have millions of users and operate at scale. There are also many other companies now that provide many services online. Identification and recovery of any problems quickly is crucial for these companies. In the modern world, any issue with a service not only leads to a revenue impact but a reputational impact as users post the issues in social media like Twitter. Hence, the larger that the MTTD and MTTR is, the greater is the revenue and reputational impact.

The following are a few examples of outages that have occurred in the past. These suggest that the importance of detection and recovery should be as soon as technically possible.

- In 2015, there was an outage at a major online services provider that lasted for many hours and this impacted multiple services of it. The estimated revenue loss was about $20 MM.

- In 2016, there was a power outage in the data center of an airlines that resulted in the cancellation of certain flights. The estimated revenue loss was about $100 MM.
- In 2019, there was an outage at a social media company that was caused due to a configuration change that impacted its apps and services.

There are several things that can be done to reduce MTTD and MTTR which will be covered in the incident management, monitoring and alerting, observability, and DevSecOps chapters.

SRE team responsibilities

While the responsibilities of SRE teams in different companies might vary a bit, the following are some of the common responsibilities. The required knowledge and related practical examples to achieve these responsibilities are explained in this book.

- Work with business and development teams in setting the SLOs for the services that they operate.
- Set up an agreed error budget policy.
- Collaborate with development teams to ensure that the new services are being designed, developed, tested, and released to operate reliably.
- Verify the new updates to ensure that the existing services meet the requirements in the launch checklist.
- Identify inter-dependent services with different requirements of reliability.
- Eliminate toil through automation.
- Set up the required log/metrics/traces collection, log/metrics/traces storage and visualization, monitoring, alerting, and auto-remediation solutions.
- Eliminate false positives that get alerted. For example, there might be an alert that the service is down but it might not actually be down. To avoid false positives, multiple health checks are used as a combination to avoid the false positives. An example is to health check whether the service is up with its health check end-point and also check whether the user requests are being served as expected by the service from the central logs.

- Set up a mechanism to co-relate incidents that are caused by a single root problem.
- Predict failures wherever possible and even before they occur.
- Detect anomalies in service behaviour.
- Be on-call and manage incidents to handle outages.
- Monitor SLIs, SLOs, error budgets, MTTD, MTTR, and MTBF
- Conduct blameless post-mortems.
- Conduct chaos game days at regular intervals to uncover any unknown systemic weaknesses.
- Set up automations for managing existing infrastructure, and setting up and configuring new infrastructure.
- Capacity planning using forecasting algorithms to understand the future needs of the infrastructure
- Certain tools are required to meet the above responsibilities. Some of the tools are available in open source and some are available through vendors. However, given the variation in how different companies develop, deploy, and run their services, neither open source or vendor tools may be suitable. In such cases, there is a need for SREs to write a new tool of their own.
- Continuously improve the processes through learning.
- Upgrade infrastructure and tools or migrate to totally new ones since better options are available, or decide based on the change in demand for the services.

Skill set of SREs

Site reliability engineers are a unique set of resources who have both software engineering and operational knowledge. They will need to have a broad skill set, including but not limited to the following:

- Understanding of infrastructure (virtualization, provisioning, configuration, upgrades, and decommissioning)
- Containerization technology like Docker
- Infrastructure automation tools like Chef and Ansible
- Networking and Firewalls

Introduction to SRE ■ 51

- Unix/Linux internals (memory management, NAS, NFS, IO, process checks, crontab)
- TCP/IP protocol suite
- Domain Name System (DNS)
- PaaS platforms like Pivotal Cloud Foundry, OpenShift, Kubernetes, and vSphere Integrated Containers
- Cloud Services like AWS, GCP, and Microsoft Azure
- Programming experience in one or more of Python, Go, Shell, Perl, Java, and JavaScript/Angular/React
- Distributed system design
- Microservices
- Load balancers like Nginx, HAProxy, and so on.
- Web servers like Apache, Tomcat, Nginx, and so on.
- Messaging solutions like Kafka, IBM MQ, RedHat AMQ, and so on.
- Content Delivery Network (CDN)
- Automated testing
- Application and infrastructure security
- CI/CD tools like Git, Jenkins, Bamboo, Ansible, Puppet, SonarQube, Fortify, Nexus, and so on.
- Blue/green and canary deployments
- Instrumentation/logging/tracing/monitoring/telemetry/observability/alerting tools like Nagios, ELK stack, Fluentd, Jaeger, Zipkin, Prometheus, Grafana, Splunk, Datadog, AppDynamics, Zabbix, Nand so onool, PagerDuty, BigPanda, and so on.
- Change management processes
- SLIs, SLOs, and error budgets
- Incident management
- Chaos engineering
- Big data platforms like Hadoop
- Machine learning (nice to have)

Conclusion

In this chapter, you have learnt how the DevOps framework is put into practice by implementing SRE. An introduction to the key focus areas of SRE was provided and will be explained in much more detail throughout the length of this book.

In the next chapter, you will learn how one of the core preaching of DevOps—automation is put into practice by SRE. You will be provided with an explanation on what toil is and how it can be identified. Also, you will learn how once the toil is identified, it can be either eliminated or reduced to improve operational efficiency.

Multiple choice questions

1. **The following is a not a term coined as part of SRE evolutions.**
    a) SLA
    b) SLI
    c) SLO
    d) Error budget

2. **Measured over a period of time, SREs ensure that:**
    a) SLI < SLO
    b) SLI > SLO
    c) SLI is better than SLO
    d) None of the above

Answers
1. a
2. c

Chapter 4
Identify and Eliminate Toil

Every service in an IT organization has a support structure which is built up of layers. Individuals with different levels of expertise are present in this support structure and tapped into as required by the applications. The teams are also often organized based on the expertise level of the support required. Generally, teams that are often the first touch point for any issue or outage in the services and take a first stab at resolving the issue are referred to as L1/L2 teams. Based on the complexity of the issue, individuals with higher level of expertise are involved in troubleshooting any issues or for executing a task or project. These individuals are referred to as L3/L4 resources.

Structure

In this chapter, we will discuss the following topics:

- Understanding toil
- Process optimization with automation
- Examples of toil with approaches to automate them

Objective

In this chapter, you will learn what toil is and what are the different types of work that are classified as toil. You will learn about the process of identifying toil and systematically eliminating it wherever needed with the help of some real-life use cases.

Understanding toil

The two key areas that the IT support teams are expected to deliver on are as follows:

- Ensuring that the services are running at the agreed level
- Deploying and upgrading services and systems without causing outages to the service

In order to efficiently execute the two responsibilities listed, the IT support teams have to ensure that they take care of multiple housekeeping jobs on a daily basis. Often, these jobs are executed manually. Also, the nature of many of these tasks is very static and seldom does it need a fresh approach or a problem-solving technique which demands the full attention of a human. As time passes, in organizations, these types of jobs tend to pile up and consume a lot of employee time, which is taxing for the organization.

Apart from the actual technical work that the teams deliver on, there is also administrative work; for example, HR related work, team collaboration related work, and so on. It is important to understand that while this work might be manual and could also be repetitive, it is clearly not directly related to running a production service.

An organization can develop its own process to categorize any tasks into toil by creating a checklist of attributes that the task checks against. This check list can be as follows:

- Repetitive work which contributes to running a production service
- Manually implemented
- Can be automated with no human processing needed to execute
- Linearly scales with service

If any task displays the above-mentioned traits, then it can be considered as toil and is a good candidate for automation. An efficient IT team is good at recognizing these kinds of jobs and automating them.

Importance of eliminating toil

A modern-day IT team is expected to continuously improve and upskill itself. The biggest problem with an organization that is carrying a large amount of toil is the effect that it has on the growth of the individuals within its IT teams. Executing work that is actually toil day in and day out can give the individuals a false sense of accomplishment wherein they have achieved mastery over their craft. They tend to get into a comfort zone which becomes difficult to break away from. As time goes by, they keep isolating themselves from other areas. This has a domino effect on many other areas within IT. There is challenge in taking anything without adding more headcount to the team as the current members are always busy toiling away.

Introducing a new technology also gets very difficult as the teams develop an affection to the existing technology and processes, and find it very difficult to break away from them. Not having enough time to learn something new because of toil keeping them busy is another reason contributing to this.

For an organization to keep evolving and improving itself, they have to keep shedding any dead weight they might be carrying in the form of toil. The more toil you can eliminate, the more new and challenging work you can move towards. Effectively running this cycle of identifying toil, eliminating toil, and taking on new work are very crucial for organizations to stay relevant and to be able to beat the competition.

Process optimization with automation

By now, you should have a good idea of how to identify and isolate tasks and processes which can be classified as toil from the complete set of work that is executed by the IT teams. The obvious next step that one can think of once toil is identified is to eliminate it by means of automating the tasks. While there might be an urge to get started with the automation; in many cases, it makes sense to a step back and analyze the task in its entirety. What this means is that it is not a good practice to automate a manual process in its current state.

Before you make a decision about how to optimize a task (or process) to make it less taxing on the organization, it pays to spend time on it to understand the following aspects:

- The purpose of the task and the outcome expected.
- Any redundant steps that are being executed which can be considered as not required.
- Manual time spent on the task which includes any inactive time spent between handover among teams.

Once you gather this information, you should then start working on a plan to optimize the toil. This can be a two-step process:

1. Removing any steps that are not required and making the process lean
2. Automating the process

While the steps to automate are different for each process, having a standard framework for automation which is led by a specialist automation team is an approach which works very effectively.

In the next section, you will learn more about automation through some real-life examples.

Examples of toil with approaches to automate

There are a number of tasks that are required to be performed to operate an application/service. Some of these will be toil and need to be automated. If you are from an operations background, you can relate to some of the examples mentioned below.

Purging and archiving of files

Purging refers to the process of deleting old content. This may be files from file system, data from database, and so on. In certain cases, the old content cannot be deleted permanently but will be required to be stored elsewhere before being deleted from the original location. This is usually to meet auditing requirements. There will be various regulatory or internal auditing requirements due to which the data needs to be archived instead of being deleted permanently.

There are different types of files that are generated and/or consumed by applications. The following are some of these files and what needs to be regularly done for them.

Log files

Irrespective of the programming language, the application/service code or its associated scripts will write the log files. These log files will need to be purged/deleted to save space. The retention period may be three days or seven days but there will be no need of these beyond that period. These can be found and deleted with a simple command which is as follows:

```
find /app/xyz/logs -type f -mtime +3 -exec rm -f {} \;
```

On a daily basis, these can be archived before deleting. In such cases, files have to be archived and then deleted.

```
find /app/xyz/logs -type f -mtime +1 -exec mv {} /archive \;

find /app/xyz/archive -type f -mtime +3 -exec rm -f {} \;
```

To avoid running these manually regularly, these commands can be kept in a shell script and scheduled in cron jobs. The following is a shell script that takes the source and archive directories as input and performs the job of archiving. It takes care of error handling and is also written in a generic way that it can be re-used for any combination of source and archive directories by passing them as parameters.

```
#!/bin/bash

# Log file to capture the different steps and any errors
while running this script.
logFile=/tmp/purge.log.$(date '+%Y-%m-%d')

if [ $# != 2 ]; then
        echo "ERROR: Usage: purge.sh <source directory> <archive directory>" | tee $logFile
```

```
        exit 1
fi

sourceDir=$1
targetDir=$2

# Verify if the directories exist
if [ ! -d $sourceDir ]; then
        echo "`date`: ERROR: $sourceDir does not exist" | tee $logFile
        exit 2
fi

if [! -d $targetDir ]; then
        echo "`date`: ERROR: $targetDir does not exist" | tee $logFile
        exit 3
fi

# Find command is used with move command to move the files to target directory
find $sourceDir -type f -mtime +3 -exec mv {} $targetDir \;

if [ $? != 0 ]; then
        echo "`date`: ERROR: Error occurred while archiving log files" | tee $logFile
        exit 4
else
        echo "`date`: INFO: Successfully archived log files" | tee $logFile
fi
```

Data files

The data files may be generated by an application or received from another application. Once processed, there will ideally not be a need for these. However, in certain fields like banking, there are requirements from regulators to store them for multiple years. In these cases, the files are purged from the file system, but at the same time, they are backed up either in a tape or some other large data store.

Temp files

There are some temporary files that are generated during processing and these need to be deleted on a regular basis. These files can be deleted by writing script as shown above. This script to delete temp files by taking a directory and temp file name pattern as inputs is left as an exercise for the reader.

Purging of database tables

Similar to old files that can be purged from the file system, there is a need to purge database tables after the rows are processed or there is data that is no longer needed. It is common that when applications are developed, the purge part is missed out on since the development team is focused on building new features with the effort spent on writing the required rows and performing the required processing for user expected functionality. The following is a stored procedure in the SQL server that can be used to purge a sample table called transactions that is used to hold certain transaction data that can be deleted after about three months. The procedure deletes a maximum of 1000 rows in an iteration to avoid the filling up of a transaction log by large number of deletes.

```
CREATE PROCEDURE purge_data
AS
BEGIN

DECLARE @deleted_rows INT

SET @deleted_rows = 1

WHILE @deleted_rows > 0
BEGIN
/* Opening a transaction to commit or rollback later */
  BEGIN TRANSACTION

  DELETE TOP (1000) FROM transactions WHERE processed_date
> DATEDIFF(dd,-90,@getdate())

/* @@error is a global variable that holds error code if
```

```
previous statement fails */
  IF @@error !=0
  BEGIN
    ROLLBACK TRANSACTION
    RETURN -1
  END

/* @@rowcount is another global variable that holds number
of rows affected from previous statement */
  SET @deleted_rows = @@ROWCOUNT

  COMMIT TRANSACTION

/* Wait for 5 seconds so that log does not get full with
continuous deletes */
  WAITFOR DELAY '00:00:05'

END

RETURN 0

END
```

Installation/Patching

There will be different reasons to install new software or update software on servers. This can be a simple case of applying an update/patch for the operating system, upgrading the security software, installing databases nor database clients, and so on. These tasks can be automated by an automation tool like Ansible instead of manually copying the software binary to each server, logging in to the servers and running the installs/upgrades. The following are two ansible playbooks to copy the package file to remote and execute a script to install it.

Playbook to copy file to target servers. This will copy the content from the source directory to the **/tmp** folder on the target.

```
- hosts: all
  tasks:
    - name: copy file to remote server
      copy:
```

```
          src: /home/updates/
          dest: /tmp
```

Playbook to copy the upgrade script and execute it. This will copy the script upgrade.sh to all the target hosts and run the script.

```
- hosts: all
  sudo: true
  tasks:
    - script: /tmp/upgrade.sh
```

```
ansible-playbook upgrade.yml --user=root
```

Monitoring

In simple terms, monitoring is the process of checking whether the services and/or databases and the infrastructure are healthy and secured. It is practically not possible to regularly check whether a service is healthy or not. The difficulty in monitoring increases with an increase in the number of services and number of instances of each of the running service. Different tools are used to monitor and visualize the production infrastructure and services like Grafana, Prometheus, Nagios, Elastic Stack, and so on.

It is also common for SREs to set up scripts or other mechanisms like probes to identify and send alerts in addition to visual dashboards. The alerts can be sent to Slack channels, emails, SMS, and so on. in case there is an issue with the services or their runtimes or the network.

The following are some of the issues for monitoring and alerting that are set up.

- The service issue can be related to the service consuming a high amount of CPU, high memory, high IO, process getting hung, and so on.

- The runtime environment issue can be for scenarios like hardware failures or an issue with the components of PaaS platforms like PCF, Kubernetes, and so on.

- Network issues can be issues like latency in network, security configuration issue, and so on.

In *Chapter 7: IT monitoring* and *Chapter 8: Observability*, monitoring and related tools will be explained in detail.

Checking log files

When there is an issue with a service, one of the immediate reactions of SREs would be to check the log file for the service. However, the effort to find where the service is running, logging to the server if it is a virtual machine and checking the actual log file is a process that can be automated. The complexity further increases when the application services are running inside containers that are deployed on container orchestration platforms like Kubernetes, OpenShift, Pivotal Container Service, Swarm and so on. The solution is to send the service logs to a central location where SREs can check the logs of all services.

The following are a few ways to achieve this task for SREs:

- Run a tool called FileBeat that can collect specific patterns of log lines and send it to the ElasticSearch database.

- Run Fluentd as a central process that can collect logs from different sources, for example, using REST API calls. Fluentd can then send logs to relevant source.

- In a micro-services architecture, use an additional service called Sidecar that is attached to each service and can take care of the log collection and send it to a central location.

- For platforms like Pivotal Cloud Foundry, it provides a component called Firehose. Firehose Nozzles can be used to collect logs and metric information for services running on PCF. The collected logs can be stored in a central location; for example, the ElasticSearch database.

In one of the later chapters, these tools used to collect logs and store logs in a central location will be explained in detail.

Identify and Access Management

Identity and access management (IAM) refers to a set of processes and tools used to control the access to organization resources. Restrictions can be placed on accessing virtual machines, cloud infrastructure services, application software, databases, and so on. Single sign-on like Microsoft Azure **Active Directory** (**AD**) service, Auth0, Okta Workforce Identity, and so on. and multi-factor authentication like Cisco 2FA, RSA SecurID 2FA, and so on. are used to validate the access of a resource by a user.

Once a user is authenticated with single sign-on or multi-factor authentication, the next step is to be validated about whether the authenticated user is authorized to access a specific resource or perform an action on the specific resource. There are different ways to achieve this such as—by using AD groups, maintaining roles inside the resource and mapping users to specific roles, and so on. The toil involved for SREs would be in adding and deleting the users for the authorization part while the security team at the organization level maintains the authentication of the users. SREs make use of automation to simplify the authorization process.

- A self-service portal which internally integrates with different resources like version control software, virtual machines, databases, application services, and so on. Users can raise requests on the portal to add themselves.

- Create APIs and expose to organization onboarding portals for the resources managed by the SREs.

- While a conscious effort is put by users to raise the access to resources, there is usually no specific process while offboarding themselves. For example, on termination from the organization. SREs can create webhooks which can be integrated with single sign-on systems so that users are removed when they are removed from single sign-on systems.

The following is an example of creating a subscription using Microsoft graph API for receiving notifications whenever there are changes to a particular AD group. The webhook in **notificationUrl** is called whenever there is a change to the AD group **<group id>**.

```
https://graph.microsoft.com/v1.0/subscriptions

Content-Type: application/json
{
  "changeType": "created,updated,deleted",
  "notificationUrl": "<SRE Team Webhook URL",
  "resource": "/groups/<group id>",
```

```
    "expirationDateTime": "2021-12-31T11:00:00.0000000Z",
    "clientState": "Secrand so onlientState"
}
```

SREs can also create end of the batch jobs to reconcile with single sign-on systems. For example, Azure maintains activity log for actions done to users and user groups. The activity log can be retrieved using PowerShell commands, Azure CLI, or REST API.

Vulnerability scans

In the current world, it is utmost important to regularly scan for infrastructure and services for security. There are a variety of hackers now who try to find ways to make use of security vulnerabilities to steal data and sell it to other parties, take hold of databases and release them in exchange of bitcoins, and so on. Vulnerability scans are run to identify if there are any processes or infrastructure components with a security risk. Vulnerability scans are also run for application code and container images. As new security vulnerabilities are identified in the tech world, a quick analysis needs to be performed to assess the risk of newly identified vulnerabilities in the organization. While scans for newly identified vulnerabilities will need some new effort to update the scan scripts/scan software from vendors, vulnerability scans for known scenarios are automated and regularly run across the infrastructure.

Vulnerability scans for application code, binaries, or container images are run whenever they are deployed. In one of the later chapters, a detailed explanation is provided on infrastructure and application security.

Infrastructure provisioning/ decommissioning

In our current API / SDK / CLI driven world, provisioning and decommissioning of certain infrastructure resources can be programmatically done. For example, in the case of Amazon Web Services (AWS), there are SDKs available in different programming languages to create, configure, and manage AWS services. Boto is one such example of SDK for Python. With Boto, the current version being 3.x, EC2, and S3 resources can be created and terminated.

The following are simple steps to use Boto3.

Install boto3

Installation of boto3 requires installing the **awscli** and **boto3** packages. This can be done using the **pip** command.

```
pip install awscli boto3
```

Create EC2 instances

New EC2 instances can be created by using the resource type as EC2 and using the **create_instances** function by passing details of the AWS image ID, the number of instances to be created, and the type of EC2 instance. The following is an example to get one EC2 instance of type **t2.micro**.

This code will import the boto3 package installed above and set the resource type to **ec2**. The image id is the image id and a sample image id is used for the example purpose.

```
import boto3
ec2 = boto3.resource('ec2')

newInstance = ec2.create_instances(ImageId='ami-vvcexample 123',MinCount=1,MaxCount=1,InstanceType='t2.micro')
```

Terminate EC2 instances

The advantage with hosting on cloud is that the procured services can be terminated when they are not needed. The following is an example of terminating 3 EC2 instances using Boto3.

```
import boto3
ec2IDs = ['ec21','ec22', 'ec23']
ec2 = boto3.resource('ec2')
ec2.instances.filter(InstanceIds = ec2IDs).terminate()
```

Incident management

Incident in the IT world is a disruption to a production service or its underlying infrastructure. Incident management is the most critical task of SREs. A lot of work is done, right from designing a service to running and monitoring it to ensuring that it does not get disrupted. Alerts are set up to notify when it starts getting disrupted but there are still some things that happen which need a human to analyze. Production incidents can lead to significant revenue loss for organizations. Due to the level of impact that an incident can have on organizations, advanced machine learning techniques are now being used to predict them even before they occur. There are different types of incidents that occur. For example:

- A service gets completely down.
- There is a reduction in the quality of the service in terms of performance or expected functionality.
- The service is hung.
- Long running queries causing deadlocks or other queries get stuck.
- The virtual machine is not reachable.
- Hardware failures like RAM or disk failure.
- Reduction in quality in an external service with cascading effect to an internal service.
- Issue with components of orchestration platforms.

When an incident occurs, there are different steps that are performed. These are as follows:

- Triage of the issue.
- Escalation to another team if the source of the problem is elsewhere.
- Escalation to different levels of management based on the severity of the incident.
- Regular communication with internal teams and management.
- External communication if external users are impacted.
- Resolution and restoring the service to its normal state.
- Post-mortem of the incident to see if can be avoided in the future or if the impact can be reduced.

The following diagrams explain the above flow in terms of handling the incident and the related communication for high severity incidents.

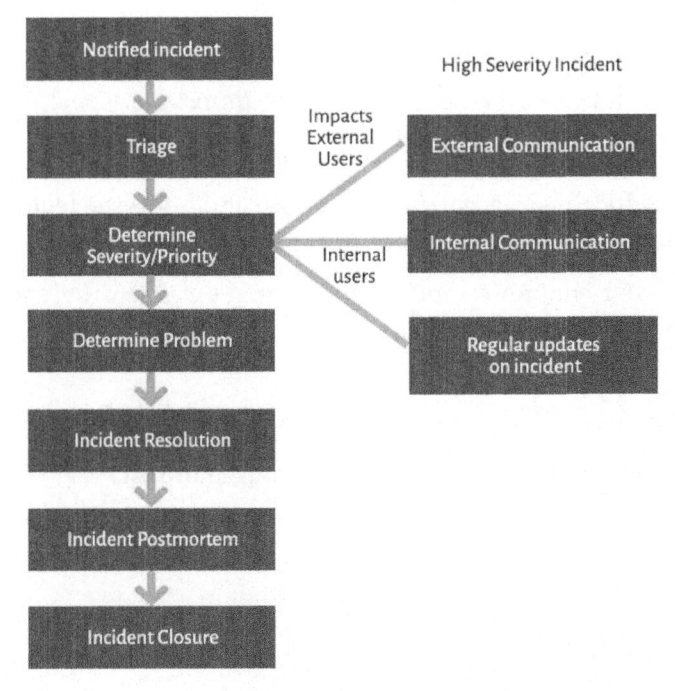

Figure 4.1

There are different types of automation that can be done in incident management space. For example:

- Automatically restarting a service that crashes
- Automated fail over
- Detecting and automatically remediating a potential security threat
- Automatically changing router config to route traffic to healthy services
- Automated routing of incidents to relevant SREs
- Automatically relating to a previous incident using natural language processing techniques based on initial analysis
- Sending alerts to on-call SREs
- Maintaining a central tool for end-to-end tracking of incident

Conclusion

Eliminating toil can prove to be an important aspect of optimizing operations. A site reliability engineer should commit to constantly eliminating toil. Having a weekly checkpoint to assess the amount of toil reduced is a very fruitful exercise and helps the teams to keep on taking up newer challenges.

In a later chapter on incident management, the different techniques will be explained.

Multiple choice questions

1. **The following is not an example of toil.**
   a) Logging into multiple servers to check log files to analyze issues.
   b) Patching of multiple virtual machines
   c) Hiring process
   d) Automated alerting

2. **Toil is any work that is:**
   a) Manual
   b) Repetitive
   c) Linearly scales
   d) All of the above

3. **The following is an example tool used for log collection.**
   a) Filebeat
   b) Boto
   c) Grafana
   d) Kibana

Answers

1. c
2. d
3. a

Chapter 5
Release Management

The world today has become more and more dependent on digital services and the expectations of the consumers of these digital services keep increasing as well. This has brought a whole new challenge to the software development area. The product owners have to understand the pulse of the consumers and have to be in a position to steer the product in the direction of the consumers expectations. For this to happen, the traditional waterfall model of software development process will not work mainly because a product can no longer wait till a 3-month (or more) period to bring in new features.

Releasing code as early and as often as possible is considered to be a very important practice that needs to be followed for a modern-day product to stay alive. This helps the software not only to stay aligned with the user's expectations but also enables building quality products as bugs are addressed almost immediately once they are reported.

Release engineering comprises a set of practices which are followed to package the code that is written by the software developers and delivering it as a final product to its users.

Structure

In this chapter, we will discuss the following topics:

- Understanding release management
- Release automation with CI/CD
- Blue-green deployments
- Canary deployments

Objective

In order to release software frequently, there are a set of practices that need to be followed which have emerged as release patterns over time. A solid software release practice which includes **CI/CD (continuous integration, continuous deployment/delivery)** automation is the best way to ensure smooth and frequent release of software. The popular methods, practices, and frameworks that are followed by release engineers across the globe to deliver software in a timely manner with minimum disruption will be introduced in this chapter. You will also learn about the practice of Infrastructure as Code for optimizing operational work like configuration management. It helps in automating a repeated standard way of work.

Understanding release management

The scope of release management spans over almost all of the software development lifecycle stages. The release engineering team is a separate team in organizations whose responsibility is to work closely with the software developers and finalize all the steps that will be followed for releasing the software. This process involves determining the source code repository to be used and the structure that should be followed in the repository to manage the code effectively, building the workflow for releasing software which consists of the different checkpoints, or gates that govern the flow of the code towards a release, and the testing and security scans that should be embedded within the release workflow.

In practice, the final workflow built for releasing products may vary for different organizations and even within an organization, it might vary for different products, but most release management processes follow the following steps as captured in the following figure:

Figure 5.1

Release planning

Planning a release tends to be an intensive exercise as it is done at the early stages of the product development lifecycle and there are many unknowns that need to be anticipated and incorporated into the plan. This phase also needs coordination between the development and the release team to determine the final workflow which needs to incorporate the change management process, build tools and technologies, timelines and quality gates to be incorporated in the build workflow.

Build package

Based on the release plan, the build workflows are implemented, and the code has to be built into the applications that are in a ready-to-be-tested state. Mostly, implementing the build process is a one-time activity if there are best practices like separation of code and configuration followed.

Test for quality and security

Once a build package is ready, it is deployed to a test environment where it is subjected to different types of quality checks as well as security scans which have been identified as per the release plan. The build and test phase in the release cycle are often performed multiple times before the release can be delivered based on the results of the tests and scans. The standard of release quality is often determined at the time of the release plan, and until the build package meets these quality requirements, it is not allowed to pass through this phase. The detailed requirements are explained under the *Launch Checklist* topic of the book.

Deployment

If a build is able to pass through the quality checks, it is deemed ready to be pushed to the users and is deployed to the production environment. Depending on the magnitude of the release (major, minor), specific plans for the release need to be put into place which could range from awareness to the users of the product on 'what is new to expect' and keeping the support team ready to handle any challenges or queries on the new release.

The release engineering practice becomes a very important piece of delivering the software service as it is responsible for continuously delivering the software by following a standard set of practices which can be repeated any number of times without any change in the process followed for software delivery.

Release automation with CI/CD

As consumers keep using digital services, their capability to ingest the services and their reliance on these services also keeps growing. This also increases their appetite for new features and in many cases, they are not willing to wait a long time for these new features to be made available to them.

For organizations to cope up with the requirements for scaling up their software delivery, the automation of release engineering practice is an important step. This automation of release consists of automating the build and deployment practices which are also known as CI or continuous integration and CD or continuous deployment or delivery.

Continuous integration refers to the automation practice of developers checking-in their code update to a common or main branch of the source code repository which is then merged with code pushed by other developers. As a best practice, the code is often also subjected to scans conducted by code quality / security tools triggered by webhooks implemented within the code repository to ensure that there are no vulnerabilities introduced by the new code and the code is of high quality.

Once the new code is successfully merged, an automated build process kicks in. The build process compiles the code into binaries which are then deployed to a test environment. The built package also gets scanned for security and tested for functionality. If the code manages to pass the required quality and security checks, then depending on the way the workflow is configured, it can get deployed all the way to the production environment. This process of taking a version of code and making it deployment ready is referred to as continuous deployment.

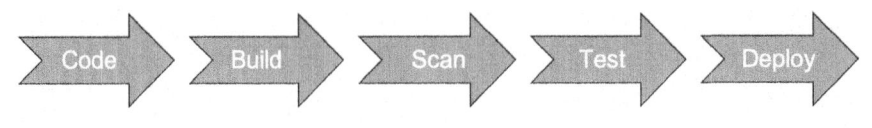

Code → Build → Scan → Test → Deploy

Figure 5.2

Using IaC for release management

In organizations, a lot of effort is required in managing the infrastructure needed for delivering software services to their users. This infrastructure mainly consists of systems and network components. Until recently, most of the work in this space was conducted in a manual fashion with a team of administrators. This meant a good amount of effort was required by a large team and there was always a risk to the quality of service as a result of errors introduced by this large team doing work manually. However, things have evolved over time and there are newer practices now that are adopted to ease out these challenges and they have paved the way for effective management of infrastructure.

One such practice is the management of infrastructure required for hosting software applications by the means of the Infrastructure as Code practice. Infrastructure as Code is used to manage configuration drift which can also result in environment drift. It means that the code is deployed to a consistent environment for testing so the results of the tests conducted only give insights into the quality of the application. The results are not affected by the deviations that might have occurred into the environments between a previous release and the current release.

To implement Infrastructure as Code, teams have to get rid of any manual provisioning or configuration of infrastructure. A set of blueprints or templates are created, mostly in a JSON or YAML file format which are kept current based on any changes in conditions. Also, at no given point is any manual change to the infrastructure configuration is allowed.

Blue-green deployments

In *Chapter 2: Introduction to DevOps*, the practice of blue-green deployments was introduced. It is a practice where the newer version of the application/service is deployed on a new instance. The application/service traffic is routed to the new instance (green) after verification. The earlier version (blue) can be retained for rollback or it can be removed.

The following is an example of how blue-green deployment can be done on Kubernetes. The example here uses minikube, the tool that makes it easy to run Kubernetes on a personal computer.

Since, this is the first time in the book that we are looking at Docker and Kubernetes examples, the installation steps are also mentioned here.

The following steps are explained along with the required commands to explain how a new version can be deployed and switched dynamically.

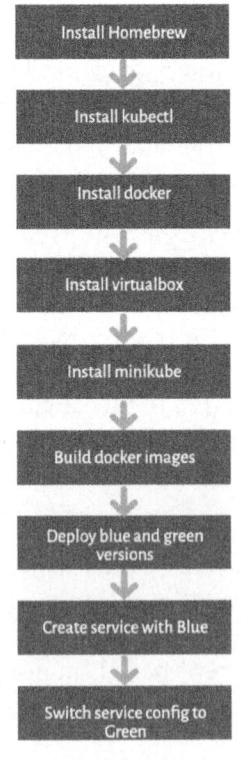

Figure 5.3

Homebrew is used to install minikube and the dependent software on Mac. Readers are suggested to look out for the installation steps for other operating systems.

The following command updates the brew version.

`brew update`

The following command installs kubectl, the command line tool for Kubernetes.

`brew install kubectl`

The following command installs Docker.

`brew cask install docker`

The following command installs VirtualBox. VirtualBox is a free and open-source hypervisor software.

`brew cask install virtualbox`

The following command installs minikube, the command line tool for Kubernetes.

`brew install minikube`

Once the installation is done, the installation can be verified by doing the version check. These are the versions at the time of writing this chapter. The versions can change while trying these at the time of you reading the book.

Checking version of docker:

```
MacBook-Air:green$ docker --version
Docker version 19.03.8, build afacb8b
Checking version of minikube:
MacBook-Air:green $ minikube version
minikube version: v1.12.1
commit: 5664228288552de9f3a446ea4f51c6f29bbdd0e0
```

Checking version of kubectl:

```
MacBook-Air:green$ kubectl version --client
Client Version: version.Info{Major:"1",
Minor:"18", GitVersion:"v1.18.6",
GitCommit:"dff82dc0de47299ab66c83c626e08b245ab19037",
GitTreeState:"clean", BuildDate:"2020-07-15T23:30:39Z",
```

```
GoVersion:"go1.14.4", Compiler:"gc", Platform:"darwin/
amd64"}
```

The source code files for this example are checked into GitHub as a public repo. The repo can be cloned by using the following clone link.

https://github.com/xfgeek/Minikube-Blue-Green-Example.git

The source code repository has two directories – blue and green. These directories represent two different versions of the web application built using the flask framework. Flask is a lightweight framework in Python to build web applications; it is further used in the examples of the book.

The Python code for the web application is in the file flask_docker_example.py and the templates folder. The difference in the two versions of the application is in the index.html folder in the templates folder. The blue version of the web application has the text **Hello Blue!** in its homepage and the green version of the web application has the text **Hello Green!** in its homepage.

This difference makes it easy to verify the version of the application being accessed from a browser in the following steps.

1. The Dockerfile in the two directories is the same and is used to build the image for the application. The following line in the Dockerfile mentions the Python version to be considered for building the image.

   FROM python:3.6.1-alpine

2. The following two commands create a directory and add the files into it from the blue or green directories respectively.

   WORKDIR /sample_image
   ADD . /sample_image

3. The following command adds the **flask** package to the image.

   RUN pip install flask

4. The following command starts the Flask application when the image is run directly using Docker or within a Kubernetes pod.

   CMD ["python","flask_docker_example.py"]

5. Each directory has the respective deployment configuration file that is used when deploying the image in a pod. The following line tells that it is used to mention the version.
   ```
   apiVersion: apps/v1
   ```

6. The following line mentions that this configuration file is a deployment configuration.
   ```
   kind: Deployment
   ```

7. The following line mentions the name that comes up as the deployment name when the `kubectl get deployment` command is run.
   ```
   metadata:
     name: flask-deployment-blue
   ```

8. The following lines mention that the number of replicas of this pod is to be 1 and labels to match this deployment in other kubectl commands.
   ```
   spec:
     replicas: 1
     selector:
       matchLabels:
         app: flask-app
     template:
       metadata:
         labels:
           app: flask-app
           role: blue
   ```

9. The following lines mention the container name, image name, and the port of the container that is to be exposed. The container can be identified with this name in the output of the **docker ps** command.
   ```
       spec:
         containers:
         - name: flask-container
           image: localhost:8080/flask-app:1.0
           ports:
           - containerPort: 5000
   ```

10. The other configuration file in the source code is **service.yml**. It is for creating the service in the Kubernetes cluster. The following line mentions the API version.

    ```
    apiVersion: v1
    ```

11. The following line mentions that this configuration file is for creating a service.

    ```
    kind: Service
    ```

12. The following line is the name used to identify the service.

    ```
    metadata:
      name: flask-app
    ```

13. The following lines mention the deployment that needs to be exposed with the service.

    ```
    spec:
      selector:
        app: flask-app
        role: blue
    ```

14. The following lines mention the port through which the service can be accessed and the port of the container.

    ```
    ports:
      - protocol: TCP
        port: 5000
        targetPort: 5000
    ```

15. The following line mentions that this service is of type **NodePort** which is a way to directly expose the container port to a network outside the Kubernetes cluster.

    ```
    type: NodePort
    ```

Once the source code from the repo is checked out, follow the steps given below to see how blue-green deployment can be achieved in Kubernetes.

1. Run the following command to start the Kubernetes cluster.

   ```
   minikube start
   ```

2. Run the following command for minikube to use the local Docker daemon.

```
eval $(minikube docker-env)
```

3. Run the following commands from the blue directory to build the Docker image for the blue version of the application.
   ```
   cd blue
   docker build -t flask-app-v1
   ```

4. Run the following commands from the green directory to build the docker image for the green version of the application.
   ```
   cd ../green
   docker build -t flask-app-v2
   ```

5. Run the following command for Kubernetes to pick the images from the local machine.
   ```
   docker run -d -p 8080:8080 --restart=always --name registry registry:2
   ```

6. Run the following commands to tag the two images built above to the local registry started by the above **docker run** command.
   ```
   docker tag flask-app-v1 localhost:8080/flask-app:1.0
   docker tag flask-app-v2 localhost:8080/flask-app:2.0
   ```

7. Run the following command to see the four images – two originally created and the two images tagged.
   ```
   docker images
   ```

8. Run the following command from the blue directory to create the deployment, pods, and replication controllers for the blue version of the application.
   ```
   kubectl apply -f blue.yml
   ```

9. Run the following command from the green directory to create the deployment, pods, and replication controllers for the green version of the application.
   ```
   kubectl apply -f green.yml
   ```

10. Run the following commands to view the deployments, pods, and replication controllers created with the two commands given above.
    ```
    kubectl get deployments
    ```

80 ■ Hands-on Site Reliability Engineering

```
kubectl get pods
kubectl get rs
```

11. Run the following command to create the service for the pods. The service is used to expose the containers outside the cluster so that they can be accessed from a browser. As seen in the preceding steps, the **service.yml** currently points to the blue version of the app.

    ```
    kubectl apply -f service.yml
    ```

12. Run the following command to view that the service is created.

    ```
    kubectl get service
    ```

13. Run the following command to view the IP and port at which the service can be accessed. You will get **127.0.0.1** as the IP address which refers to the localhost and a random port number.

    ```
    minikube service flask-app –url
    ```

14. Do a curl on the command line or view on the browser with the IP and port. This should render the index.html file from the blue version of the app as the service initially refers to the blue version of the app.

    ```
    MacBook-Air:green$ curl http://127.0.0.1:51346

    <!DOCTYPE html>
    <html lang="en">
    <head>
        <meta charset="UTF-8">
        <title>The blue app</title>
    </head>
    <body>
        <h1> Hello Blue ! </h1>
    </body>
    ```

15. Now, run the following command to switch the service to the green version of the app. As you can see, the selector includes the role of green which is in the metadata labels in the deployment file **green.yml**.

    ```
    kubectl patch svc/flask-app -p
    ```

```
'{"spec":{"selector":{"app":"flask-
app","role":"green"}}}'
```

16. Run the above curl again and the service renders the **index. html** from the green version of the app. This shows that the service is updated to use the green version of the app.

```
MacBook-Air:Kubernetes vishnu$ curl
http://127.0.0.1:51314
<!DOCTYPE html>
<html lang="en">
<head>
    <meta charset="UTF-8">
    <title>The green app</title>
</head>
<body>
    <h1> Hello Green ! </h1>
</body>
```

As we can see in the preceding example, two versions of the web applications are deployed in two different pods and a switch to the new version is done dynamically by exposing them as a service. In the real world, a live verification is run by users or SREs or in an automated fashion before switching to the new version of the service.

Similar techniques can be used, depending on the platform where the application/service is deployed. For example, for Spring Boot applications deployed on **Pivotal Cloud Foundry** (**PCF**), the routing mechanisms in PCF are used to route the traffic to different versions.

Canary deployments

Canary deployments as a practice were introduced in *Chapter 2*: *Introduction to DevOps*. In the case of canary deployments, a part of the production traffic is routed to the new version of the application/ service to verify the new version fully before the entire traffic is routed. This deployment strategy can be used when a Load Balancer is used to split the incoming traffic to the different instances. We can take the same source code as in the preceding example and make some changes to take a look at how canary deployments work.

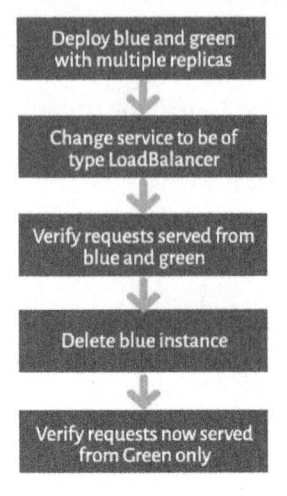

Figure 5.4

The following steps are explained along with the required commands:

1. The first step is to delete the previously running pods and service. The following commands can be used to delete them.

   ```
   kubectl delete service flask-app
   kubectl delete deployment flask-deployment-blue
   kubectl delete deployment flask-deployment-green
   ```

2. The next step is to make some changes to run multiple instances of the app. In both **blue.yml** and **green.yml**, change the number of replicas to **2**. This means that there will be two instances of version of one (blue) of the application and two instances of the version 2 (green) of the application that will be in the running status.

   ```
   replicas: 2
   ```

3. The next step is to remove the following role from the selector so that the service is used to expose both the blue and green versions.

   ```
   role: blue
   ```

   And also, change the following line to change the type of the service from **NodePort** to **LoadBalancer**. The type of **LoadBalancer** mentions to Kubernetes to start the service and distribute the incoming traffic to the running instances (pods). Out of the traffic, 50% will go to the blue instance and 50% to the green.

type: LoadBalancer

On creating the service using the same steps as mentioned above in the blue-green deployment, the service will be started and will be ready to accept requests. But since the type is **LoadBalancer**, each request is routed to a different instance. Start the service as provided in the above example for blue-green deployment and run the curl command or open from a browser. You will see the output changing from blue and green.

Since you have two replicas of both green and blue, delete the blue version of the application. This will leave only the green version of the pods behind the load balancer. Run the **curl** command or open it from a browser. You will now see responses only from the green version of the app.

kubectl delete deployment flask-deployment-blue

Depending on the type of the application and percentage of traffic to be routed to the new instance, the number of running pods for each of the versions can be varied. In a later chapter, examples are provided of other load balancers where specific configuration can be provided to mention what percentage of the traffic is to be routed to a specific instance. When using such load balancers, the traffic percentage can be controlled at the load balancer level in a different way than being based on the number of pods.

Conclusion

Release management is an important means of achieving the business goals of an organization as the maturity of the release process has a direct influence in meeting customer expectations. While it might be difficult to get the release process right the very first time that you implement, organizations tend to evolve their processes over time and find the right balance that works for them. In many other cases, even in the release process, automation forms an integral means of scaling and maintaining the quality of the release.

Having a healthy release pipeline means that the software developers and the release teams are not spending their energy on every release and can instead focus on other critical areas.

In the next chapter, you will learn about how to improve the reliability of an application or a service which is running in production by implementing effective monitoring.

Multiple Choice Questions

1. Which of the following is NOT a step in release workflow?
   a. Build
   b. Scan
   c. Monitor
   d. Test

2. Which of the following deployment approach(es) is/are used to improve the reliability of the release?
   a. Blue-green deployment
   b. Canary deployment
   c. Automated rollback
   d. All of the above

3. Which of the following is/are created when a deployment is applied in Kubernetes?
   a. Deployment
   b. Pod
   c. Replication controller
   d. All of the above

Answers

1. c
2. d
3. d

CHAPTER 6
Incident Management

No matter how well an application is architected and built, there will be situations where it will fail. After all, the SRE mindset is about accepting failure as normal. These failures can be in the form of the application services not being available such as processing user requests, background jobs, data transfers between services, and so on. Incident management is about managing these failures, right from identifying the incident to restoring any impacted services and following it up with an investigative process which will help in preventing the recurrence of the incident.

Structure

In this chapter, we will discuss the following topics:

- Understanding incident management
- Blameless postmortems
- Incident example
- Incident knowledge base
- Role of development teams

Objective

This chapter covers the various steps, mechanisms, processes, and terms in incident management. You will develop an understanding of what it takes to provide a reliable software service and how to maintain business continuity, knowing the obvious which is that services are bound to fail. If you ever need to be on-call in the future or want to improve your current process, this chapter will have what you need.

Understanding an incident management

Every modern-day organization is dependent on a number of software services that either support its internal operations or support its business functions. Some of these services can be very critical to the organizations while others are more of enablers. Nevertheless, every service has a role to play and more or less contributes to the proper functioning of an organization.

Incident

Painting with a broad brush, it can be stated that *an event that causes a disruption to a service or the operations of an organization can be termed as an incident*. A few properties that can be attributed to an incident are as follows:

- An incident is unplanned.
- An incident can be contextual which means it could occur due to various possibilities coming together to cause it.
- It can be misleading to its pursuers as it surfaces as a symptom which might not directly point to the cause.
- It may or may not be persistent until fixed and can be difficult to reproduce.

Incident management is the process followed by IT teams to respond to an event that has occurred in the environments they support, to minimize the damage it continues to cause, and to restore any services that have been fully or partially impacted.

Incident lifecycle

An incident typically moves through many phases from its inception to closure. The major states that constitute an incident's lifecycle are explained as follows:

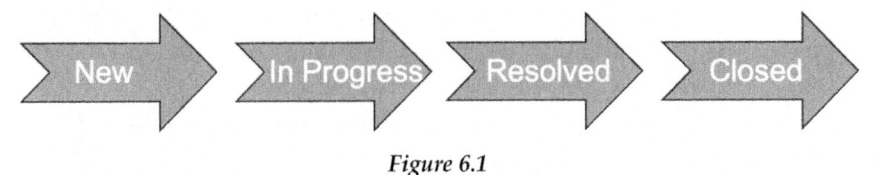

>> New >> In Progress >> Resolved >> Closed >>

Figure 6.1

The following is the explanation for the preceding figure:

- **New**: An incident is considered to be in "new" state if it has been detected but has not yet been triaged upon. Once an incident enters the new state, the clock starts ticking in terms of the metrics that are typically captured to measure the time taken for the incident to be resolved once it's detected.

- **In progress**: Once an incident is assigned for remediation and is started to be worked upon towards resolution, it is considered to be **in progress** state.

- **Hold**: If during the process of triaging the incident, there is a handover of the ownership of the incident remediation from one individual or team to another individual or team, it might be put on a **hold** status. Also, an incident might be put on a **hold** status if there is a dependency that needs to be resolved without which it is not possible to continue pursuing the resolution process of the incident.

- **Resolved**: If the incident is successfully remediated, then it is considered to be in the **resolved** state.

- **Closed**: If the incident remains in the **resolved** state for a specific time period and is no longer causing any impact to the service or operations, it is considered as **closed**.

Incidents are also closed if they are created due to false alerts. False alerts are flagged due to a misinterpretation of the service state.

Blameless postmortems

Once an incident is closed, in many organizations, a post process is executed which is considered as a retrospective or a post-mortem of the incident. Traditionally, the goal of this practice used to be to identify who and what caused the incident so as to not have a repeat of the incident and also reprimand the responsible people for causing it. This practice tends to create a sense of insecurity among the teams as there is an element of public shaming that they undergo in front of their peers and there is in certain cases an act of facing the punishment for causing the incident. This sometimes results in individuals keeping things to themselves and not sharing all the required information which is detrimental to building resiliency in the services.

In order to overcome this challenge, the SREs have come up with the concept of blameless postmortems. Postmortems are meetings where members from multiple teams come together and go through the details of the incident in order to come up with a plan to ensure that the incident never recurs. The essence of blameless postmortems can be related to retrospectives in Agile practice and can be very well captured by the following statement:

"Regardless of what we discover, we understand and truly believe that everyone did the best job they could, given what they knew at the time, their skills and abilities, the resources available, and the situation at hand."

--Norm Kerth, Project Retrospectives: A Handbook for Team Review

Although it appears to be straightforward, practicing the directive stated above is not always understood by everyone. A clear guideline to follow during the postmortems is to never corner any individual into confessing to his/her faults that had resulted in causing the incident. This tends to be very difficult because as humans, we are quick to point out the faults of others and their actions being the reason for causing the service outage which may have created so much trouble and trauma for all involved. Self-reflections are not often carried out successfully by many, and looking at others who can be blamed for an incident tends to be the default behavior.

The key areas to focus on for running successful retrospections are as follows:

- Having a neutral facilitator to open up the discussion and run through the retrospections, thereby always driving the discussions towards identifying what can be improved to build more resiliency in the affected service.
- Creating a safe environment where everyone has a voice and can be heard.

It takes a lot of practice and dedication to achieve mastery in the art of running blameless retrospections successfully and organizations need to believe that this process will drive the necessary behavior change in the teams and elevate the resiliency posture of their services.

Incident example

In this section, let's learn incident management through an incident example. You will learn about the incident by going through the incident lifecycle, teams/people involved, communication processes, and post-mortem/retrospectives. As an example, consider a case of a travel agency whose booking website is down.

Incident detection/notification

The first thing that happens is the pro-active identification of the incident through monitoring and alerting mechanisms. Or it can be based on the incident reported by an internal customer care executive who is a part of the customer service team and helps book tickets based on customer calls; or by end users who can go to the extent of posting it in social media. In the next chapter, we will look at different monitoring and alerting mechanisms. SREs use monitoring and alerting mechanisms to pro-actively detect incidents like this where there are availability issues. Also, in the AIOps chapter, we will look at the usage of AI to predict and detect incidents. Waiting for the issue to be identified and notified by the end users will lead to a reputational impact to the business.

In either of the ways of the incident coming into light, the incident gets assigned to the on-call SREs.

Incident triage

The next step for the incident is to analyze whether the issue still exists or if it was an intermittent or one-off issue. So, the first step that the on-call engineer should take is to check if the website is accessible to him/her. If it is not accessible, then it is a major issue; but if it is accessible, the next logical step to try this within the company firewall. For example, using the direct IP address of the virtual machine and outside the firewall using the actual domain name.

Let's say that if it is accessible within the firewall but not outside the firewall, the issue must be due to a changed firewall rule.

If it is accessible both within and outside the firewall, then the next logical step to check if it is intermittent by trying multiple times. If there is no issue, the next step varies based on the size of the travel website. Now assume that this is a large international travel website. The next possible step to check if it is an issue for a specific region or across regions. These checks actually continue until the issue is nailed down.

This flow of steps can be viewed in the following diagram:

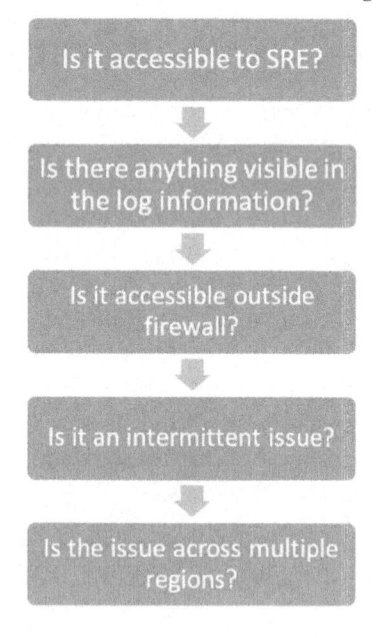

- Is it accessible to SRE?
- Is there anything visible in the log information?
- Is it accessible outside firewall?
- Is it an intermittent issue?
- Is the issue across multiple regions?

Figure 6.2

In this example, let's assume the website was not accessible by the on-call SRE as well. This is a major issue as the website is reported and also validated to be down. The next thing the on-call SRE would do is to create an incident ticket in an incident management system. There are various tools that can be used for this like JIRA, OpsGenie, Remedy, Dispatch, and so on.

While creating the ticket, there are two important categorizations that need to be decided on.

Incident severity

In general, incidents are categorized into four levels of severity.

- **Severity 1**: Incidents that cause an impact to all customers are categorized as severity 1. These are also referred to as critical incidents. Severity 1 incidents can also be attributed to severe data loss or data breaches.

- **Severity 2**: Incidents that cause impact to a large number of customers are categorized as severity 2. These are also referred to as major incidents.

- **Severity 3**: Incidents that cause impact to a small number of customers are categorized as severity 3. These are also referred to as minor incidents. For example, this can be issue about accessing the website by 1 region out of 50 regions used by the website.

- **Severity 4**: Incidents that have a minor impact with a workaround, that is, business can continue without disruption for even the small set of customers. For example, consider a small case where customers cannot book via the website but they can book via the mobile app in a specific region. This can be considered as severity 4.

Incident priority

Response to incidents depends on the priority in addition to the severity. Incidents priority is usually categorized into four levels.

- **Critical**: A critical incident needs to be resolved with the highest focus. This includes an issue that needs to be fixed almost immediately.

- **High**: A high priority incident is required to be fixed but can wait if there is a critical incident waiting to be resolved.

- **Medium**: Medium priority incidents are picked up after the high priority incidents are resolved. These are also the type of incidents given to SREs who are still learning the system, or to SREs who are learning the technology as well.
- **Low**: Low priority incidents are picked up as time permits and are also the type of incidents assigned to SREs who just joined the team or junior SREs who are new to the industry.

While it may look like severity and priority are directly proportional to the impact to the customers, it is not always related in that way.

For example, there may be a new feature that is launched and is yet to be used by the customers but is not working as expected in production. This is not a severe incident based on the number of customers impacted but this may be critical for the business to get adoption for the newly launched feature.

Coming back to our example, this is a severity 1 incident with the priority set as critical.

Incident communication

On creating the incident or while it is created, the incident is intimated to the incident commander based on the severity. In this particular example, the incident requires an incident commander to be involved. The role of the incident commander is to involve the right teams for the resolution of the incident and also to communicate to the stakeholders and/or customers.

In this example, the incident impacts external customers and there is a need to post updates in social media channels like Facebook, Twitter, and so on. Based on company policies, there might be another role/team involved in posting updates to external customers. The incident commander involves those teams as well while the incident is analyzed by SREs.

The incident commander also informs the necessary technology and business stakeholders as this is a complete downtime for the website.

The SREs and any other engineers involved in analyzing the incident can be brought together into a war room, a conference call, or into chat tools like Slack, Microsoft Teams, WhatsApp, and so on.

Incident resolution

Resolving the incident at hand is the utmost priority of the SREs. The issue might be due to one of the potential causes mentioned below. This is a small set of potential problems that can occur. There can be other causes.

- Recent release of a service that needs to be rolled back
- Recent upgrade of a database version, OS version, MQ version, and so on.
- Due to misconfiguration of a load balancer
- Incorrect DNS resolution
- A service that crashed and needs to be restarted

No matter what the reason is, the SREs analyze the cause of the problem and resolve it by restoring the website.

The resolution of the incident after identifying the issue may not always be in the hands of the SREs themselves. In certain cases, it might be a different team that needs to fix the problem; for example, the network operations.

Also, in certain organizations, there are change management processes and approval processes involved. For example, to rollback a release, an approval might be necessary from the technical product owner or the technology leadership team.

Communication is sent to the stakeholders and customers on resolving the incident.

An important thing to note about any incident at this scale is the high pressure on the SREs since any delay in resolving the incident has an impact on the revenue and reputation of the organization. The additional roles like incident commander and external communication teams are created inside organizations to let the SREs focus on resolving the technical problem as they may not effectively perform the analysis and resolution if they are distracted by the task of handling communications as well.

Just as incident notification can be done by monitoring and alerting, incident resolution can also be automated in certain cases where a resolution is known. A simple example of where automated remediation is technically possible is to restart a service which went down or restart a service which is consuming a high amount of system resources.

The metrics **mean time to detect (MTTD)** and **mean time to resolve (MTTR)** explained in *Chapter 3: Introduction to SRE* is a measure of how quickly incidents are being identified and resolved.

Incident retrospective/postmortem

After the incident is resolved, a postmortem or retrospective is conducted. SREs conduct incidents in a blameless way as explained earlier in the chapter.

An example incident retrospective is mentioned later in the section *Role of development teams* section.

Incident knowledge base

SRE teams follow the practice of maintaining the knowledge base from historical incidents. This includes the text captured on incident tickets, the root cause analysis done, and information from the retrospective meetings. The knowledge base also includes information on the terms, processes, and roles within the organization to manage incidents. This helps in analyzing the incidents in future. While there is every effort put to avoid a repeat of the same incident, they are unavoidable and can occur again. The incident knowledge base helps in quick resolutions of repeated incidents. They also help in initial checks of a similar issue in isolating the cause of the problem.

The knowledge base can be spread across multiple tools or can be pulled into a central system for easy and quick access to the information. Examples of incident management tools that help with the knowledge base are Freshservice, ZenDesk, and so on.

Role of development teams

While a number of books, blogs, or articles talk about the role of SREs or production support teams in handling the incidents, there is a role played by development teams in resolving the incidents. They are involved in incident resolution, especially when the incident is caused by one of the following:

- A recent release

- An integration issue with another application/service
- Requires analysis beyond what SREs can perform. For example, newly encountered database performance issues that need to be quickly resolved

Being a part of the development team all through my career, including a role where I was a part of the development team that built SRE products, I was involved in resolving multiple production incidents across organizations that I have worked with.

Here, I will explain an incident that I handled being part of the development.

The incident was that a portion of transactions that our application was processing were randomly failing. For the purpose of this book, let's call it application A. The key thing to note here is the random failures. The SRE team on their preliminary analysis could not find any relation for the failing transactions. They were not from the same customers, not from a particular location, not from a particular type of customers, and not for a particular type of transaction. It was just random failures and the failures were getting randomly cleared on re-processing. This was tough for the SREs as neither was there a pattern based on initial checks nor was the issue repeating for all the transactions on re-processing.

The issue in this case was handed over to the development team by the SREs for further analysis.

The development team was spread across three locations – one location in India and two locations in the US. I was the tech lead in India and there were two other leads in the US.

I was called up at 6:30 AM at Indian time to look at the problem. As a tech lead for the location, I tried to check for some time but I had no clue. So, I called up a senior developer to help me out. We both checked for a couple of hours but we still had no clue as to what the problem was. We decided to contact the primary support from our team in the US. The primary joined us to analyze the issue. We checked our code all across but couldn't figure out as there was no change in the code in the last 24 hours and everything looked fine when we were manually trying to access the data and run certain parts of the transaction which were causing failure. No issue was observed on manually checking.

After a couple of hours of checks, one thing was clear to us. There was no problem in our application and the issue had to be something to do with one of the applications we integrated with. The only common processing in all the failures was in our application and our integration point with that other application. For reference, let's call the application that I was part of as application A and the application that we integrated as application B.

By then, it was 11:30 AM in India. It had been about five hours since the incident was reported by the SRE team to me. In these five hours, I also took a break of one hour to get ready and go to office as I was logged in from home when the incident was reported. I reached the office at about 11:30 AM and then it was the turn of my senior developer to take a break and come to the office as I joined the fire fighting with the US team.

We called up the primary from the application B to help analyze the incident. While we had no real error from their application to show them to prove that the failure was coming from them, we asked them to help analyze the problem and if there were any changes on their end. Initially, they denied as we couldn't provide an actual error coming from their end. But they did start looking at it after a while.

After an hour, we let the US resources sleep as we did everything we could on our end. The time was now about 1:30 PM in India.

For us, one advantage was that we had access to the code repository of application B and their data as well. Since we did not have sufficient support from their end, my senior developer and I started analyzing their code. It wasn't our responsibility to check their code but we had no choice as our operational users were following with us.

After another five hours, at about 6:30 PM Indian time, the issue was still not identified. We looked at their code and found their changed code files in 24 hours, including the ones about which we were not sure if they were released. We learned a bit of the code of application B but there was no luck.

6:30 PM in India was 8 AM in the US location. It was then the normal starting time in the US.

The other developer and I were totally tired and mad, looking at so much code from our application A and the code from the other application B. Incidents like this also have conference calls associated with them. The call was open for almost six hours and was closed when we requested to close it as there was no point in giving an update in the call every 30 minutes. We informed the SRE team that we will let them know when we have a break through finding from our end.

As it was the normal starting time for our US tech leads, they requested for the incident call to be opened up again and then they involved the tech lead from the application B in the US. He finally found a person who had enabled logging on their calls. He did one liner change to turn it off and things were back to normal for us. It was that simple change that none of us could identify for 12 hours until the person who did the change the previous night came back online.

It was a total of 5-6 senior developers and development leads who analyzed this incident for about 12 hours until the incident was identified and resolved by the application B. It was critical in terms of priority and severity 2 in terms of severity. But it was the longest and toughest battle for me and the incident which I will probably never forget.

One week later, we conducted a postmortem for this incident. The development and support leads from both applications (application A and application B), including the senior managers for both the applications were part of the meeting. The participants in the meeting were from both India and the US, and hence, we discussed it in a conference call.

I still remember my local reporting manager pinging in the chat saying, "Welcome to the world of management escalations." It was the first escalation meeting that I had attended from India and he had sent me this message.

As a part of the meeting, what we realized was that our application A was making more than a million calls per day to application B. The application A processed transactions in batch. A batch means that our application took a number of transactions into memory and processed them at once. The main problem was later found which is that the transactions were failing when there were a number of batches being processed at the same time across our multiple processes and the overall volume exceeded a particular number. While we were checking the batch size being processed during the analysis, we had not thought of a multiplicative factor where multiple batches were being processed across processes in parallel.

There were a number of things that came out from the retrospectives of this particular incident. These are as follows:

- Neither our team nor their team knew that our application A was making so many calls to application B.
- We didn't have proper exception handling for this API call to the application B. This call was wrapped in other calls and exception handling was not set properly.
- The person who enabled logging did not inform the India team of application B of the change. It was not a standard release.
- The India team of application B denied contacting their team in the US as there was no proper error to report. Everything looked fine on normal checks and no other application integrating with them for the same data had complained. Other applications that were integrating with application B were fine as their processing volume was low. Our application A was making over a million calls per day to application B.
- The logging change in application B was not straightforward. It was a config change to enable logging and the code to perform logging was itself written and released earlier.
- There was no integration testing done with other teams after logging was enabled in application B as it was not a functional change, and it also did not appear as a change large enough to notify other teams for integration testing.

Conclusion

Incident management is not a new practice as it has existed in many organizations since a long time and has been very critical to business continuity by enabling the resolution of multiple service outages and interruptions. With the advent of newer practices like DevOps and the Agile methodology, the traditional incident management practices needed to be revamped as well. Blameless Retrospections is still an art form which is relatively new and yet to be accepted and adopted whole heartedly by most organizations. While it has its own challenges, if an organization can practice blameless retrospections successfully, it is bound to benefit from it as it has a profound impact on the culture of the organization and tends to help break down the barriers between teams and individuals.

In order to remediate incidents efficiently, it is important that you are first able to identify the incidents. In the next chapter, you will learn about implementing proactive monitoring to identify incidents as early as possible. The chapter will also cover monitoring strategies which will enable you to avoid incidents from occurring in the first place in certain cases.

Multiple choice questions

1. **Which of the following people are NOT involved in resolving incidents?**
   a. On-call SRE
   b. External communications team
   c. Project manager
   d. Incident commander

2. **Which of the following is/are the step(s) in an incident?**
   a. Incident Detection
   b. Incident Triage
   c. Incident Resolution
   d. All of the above

Answers

1. c
2. d

CHAPTER 7
IT Monitoring

A modern application's distributed and complex architecture involves multiple frontends/micro-services/functions which integrate using a variety of technologies. It is important to ensure that these services are healthy and efficient. Any interruptions in these services can be damaging to the organizations as they can have a financial and/or a brand impact. Hence, it becomes imperative that there is a solid monitoring framework in place which keeps a close watch on the overall health of the service.

Structure

In this chapter, we will discuss the following topics:

- End to end monitoring strategy
- Infrastructure monitoring
- Application monitoring
- End user monitoring
- DNS monitoring

Objective

Monitoring applications can be a daunting task because of the multiple layers that are involved for the application to work effectively. Hence, it is practically impossible to perform monitoring manually. Also, monitoring the applications is not just about identifying failures; it is also required to measure how well the application or its functionalities are being used by the end users. This chapter introduces the different concepts and techniques for monitoring the detected failures. There will be examples provided from various open-source tools to automate the monitoring of applications and software services.

End to end monitoring strategy

Monitoring has been in use by IT organizations to keep an eye on how the different components that comprise a service/application is performing. Monitoring provides insights on the health and performance of the service which typically means indicating any crashes or outages, slowness in services, and resource consumption patterns. In order to get these insights, all the different components that form a service/application need to be covered by monitoring. An application's performance can be influenced by two key categories of components — the infrastructure supporting the application and the actual application itself.

Implementing monitoring for all of the above components ensures that any glitch in a service can be identified in a timely manner, which is important when you are trying to prevent or recover from any service issues. There are multiple tools available in the market which provide monitoring capabilities on each of these areas. When evaluating and picking the right monitoring tool, it is always important that an end to end monitoring strategy is formulated by the organization.

Along with identifying the monitoring tools, a good monitoring strategy is with IT practices like the **NOC (Network Operations Center)** and the **SOC (Security Operations Center)** which determine the effectiveness of an organization's IT monitoring. While the monitoring tools are directly responsible for the **MTTD (mean time to detect** an issue), the other critical metric, which is **MTTR (mean time to repair)** is also influenced by the monitoring strategy as affective monitoring means that only relevant alerts are generated which helps the teams in focusing on resolving real issues rather than getting overwhelmed with false alarms.

A good monitoring system not only has the ability to monitor efficiently and identify anomalies, but also a solid alerting system along with good reporting capabilities.

The following image depicts what can be measured/monitored at each layer of the application and infrastructure. These will be explained in further sections in this chapter.

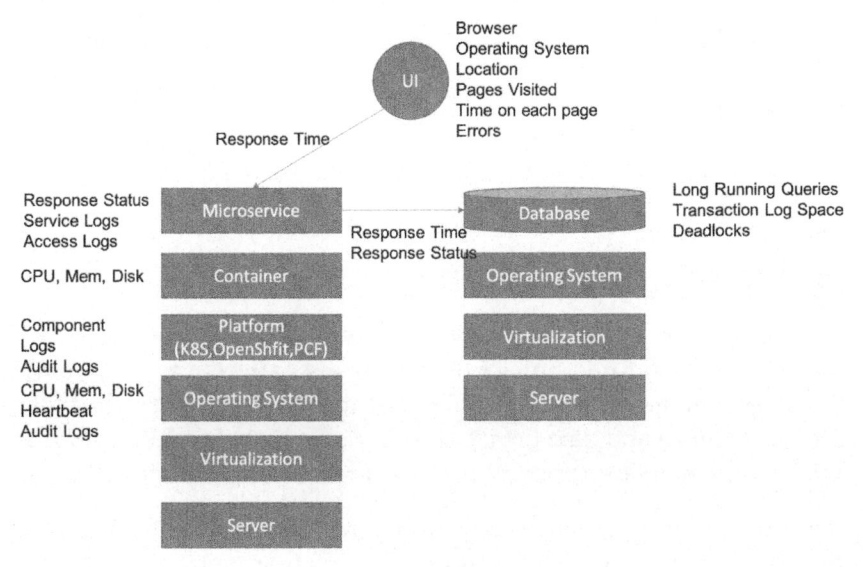

Figure 7.1

Infrastructure monitoring

Infrastructure monitoring means enabling and instrumenting the infrastructure components to generate relevant data which can be in the form of logs or documented events. The generated data can be reviewed, analyzed, and acted upon. In terms of the infrastructure components supporting an application, the key areas that contribute to providing an optimal application performance and will need to be monitored are as follows:

Server monitoring

For any service to run in a stable fashion, it is important that the server it is hosted on is performing optimally. A server should be monitored for its availability and performance. The key parameters related to any server that should be covered by a monitoring system are as follows:

- CPU utilization
- Memory utilization
- Disk I/O
- OS services
- Network interfaces
- Events and system logs

Network monitoring

Networking components form another key infrastructure area which needs to be monitored efficiently as this also affects the availability and performance of a service. An inefficient network can hurt the user experience and also brings down the security level of a service, both of which are detrimental to the organization's business.

Network monitoring is usually built on the foundation of a solid discovery model which identifies all active endpoints in the organization's environment. It has the ability to monitor all the possible routes to those endpoints and the traffic flowing through these routes. The monitoring system also performs continuous health checks on the networking components like the switches, routers, firewalls, and other network appliances which keep the connections live. As expected from any other good monitoring solution, alerting and reporting are extremely critical to efficient network monitoring.

Storage monitoring

In recent times, storage has become less expensive, and it keeps getting cheaper with time. This has resulted in organizations looking to venture into areas which involve extremely large and previously unheard of size of storage related services. Any bottlenecks or unavailability of storage services has the potential of having major impacts on the revenue. Big data related solutions are the backbone of many organizations and this makes storage an extremely valuable asset which not only needs to be secured but also needs to be running efficiently.

IOPS is often the obvious thing that needs to be monitored for a storage device. IOPS refers to the transfer time of files of to and from the storage devices in the event of a read and write operation performed by an application. All storage devices come up with a pre-defined IOPS value and they should be monitored keeping those thresholds as baseline.

The other areas to monitor on storage are the CPU utilization and the latency or the request processing time. A good storage monitoring software will provide the right level of insights into the above-stated parameters and enable the infrastructure admins to take proactive actions in a timely manner.

Application monitoring

Whether it is a traditional monolithic application or a modern micro-services-based application, SREs set up the required monitoring to identify and get notified of any issues in the application. In the earlier chapter, the concept of incident identification and notification was introduced. Setting up the right monitoring and alerting mechanisms in place helps in quick identification of problems and before the problems impact multiple users.

For reference, monolith applications contain a large amount of functionality in a small set of components. The components themselves will be very tightly coupled. On the other hand, applications built using the micro-services architecture will be built in such a way as to have smaller components/services and each of the component/service handling a specific function. In the case of micro-services, there is an ability to build and deploy each of the services differently.

Monitoring of applications is made up of a large number of micro-services requiring advanced techniques. This will be covered in *Chapter 8: Observability*. For this chapter, we will focus on the monitoring of monoliths or applications with smaller number of micro-services.

There are different problem scenarios to be identified. A few examples are as follows:

- Unavailability of a service as it is down
- Unavailability of a service as it is hung
- Processing failures identified
- Reduction in quality of the service in terms of performance or expected functionality
- Reduction in quality of a downstream application/service with a cascading effect
- Long-running queries causing deadlocks or other queries to be stuck
- Security breaches

There are a number of ways to monitor applications. These are as follows:

Probes

For services running on virtual machines directly, health check end points can be created on the services to return a 200 response when the service is healthy.

In the case of services on PaaS platforms, the PaaS platforms have in-built orchestration to do a probe check to see whether the expected number of service instances are up.

Checking logs

When developers write the code, the code is written to write different types of logs. Monitoring can be kept in place to look at log messages to identify a problem.

INFO

Logs with type INFO are written/generated for information only. These will help in checking what part of the code was getting processed and the time of processing.

DEBUG

Logs with type DEBUG do not get written/generated by default and are meant to be used while debugging and the issue in a testing environment and very rarely in production.

WARN

Logs with type WARN are warning logs written/generated.

ERROR

Logs of type ERROR are generated in any environment from development to production. These are the logs that are written/generated when there are processing errors. These errors can be due to a problem in the data being processed, a mathematical error, IO error, file system issue, an unknown error, and so on. Exceptions will need to be properly caught and written into the logs for analysis when a problem arises.

In the preceding log types, I have mentioned logs being written/generated. In case of services on virtual machines, logs will be written to log files. However, for services in PaaS platforms, logs need to be collected by other mechanisms. For example, for services deployed on Pivotal Cloud Foundry, the logs can be streamed using syslog to an external data store or they can be collected using the `cf logs` command by using the cf **CLI (command line interface)**.

For the logs that are written to log files, these can be exported to a central data store by using tools like FileBeat. FileBeat is one of the beat in Elastic Stack and can be used to watch a log file and export the lines being written into Elastic Search.

There are also mechanisms and tools for log collection that will be discussed in *Chapter 8: Observability*.

Capturing processing time

For APIs, the response time for requests is captured and logged within the code or it is captured by using other methods. The other method, for example, can be the use of Micrometer for Java applications. In either case, SREs keep a watch and get alerted if multiple requests are getting processed, more than the acceptable level.

In the case of PaaS platforms, some of them provide an in-built approach to stream response time metrics. For example, in the case of services deployed on Pivotal Cloud Foundry, metrics can be captured from what is called Firehose.

Similar monitoring is kept in place for batch jobs which run at the end of the day or multiple times a day. These jobs are usually scheduled and are not part of any online transactions. Batch jobs are set up in organizations for processes like reconciliation, profit and loss calculations for the day, file system/database clean ups, exchange of reference data between applications using flat files, and so on. Monitoring of batch jobs includes raising alerts for job failures, long running jobs, jobs which are waiting longer than expected for a dependent job or waiting for a file to be sent from another application, and so on.

MQ monitoring

Message queues are used in event-driven architectures or architectures where different components pass data between them using message queues. MQs, in simple terms, use a publisher and subscriber mechanism. Messages are pushed to what are called topics by publishers and are read by subscribers. Common problems in MQs are increasing queue depth or queue fill-ups due to slow processing by subscribers, or high volume of messages pushed by publisher, improper messages in the queue, and so on. MQs are monitored by SREs to identify these problems.

Database monitoring

I have spent half of my career working on RDBMS databases. There are some common problems that occur with RDBMS databases will need to be monitored. Some of these problems are explained in the next section.

Long running queries

One of the common hit problems with processing in databases is of long-running queries. Queries which would have worked fine before will suddenly start causing problems. This can happen due to a change in expected data in the underlying tables, an upgrade in the database version, locks held on tables by other queries, and so on. Depending on the type of the database, queries can be written by using the system tables to identify long running queries.

Long running queries would need to be identified and tuned to perform better. The performance of a query can be improved/tuned by a number of ways like creating indexes that wouldn't have been required previously, partitioning a table which has grown beyond the size that can be handled, breaking up a large query into smaller queries, avoiding co-related sub-queries, and so on.

Deadlocks

Poorly written database code or lock configuration on tables can lead to deadlocks. Deadlocks can be identified from the database logs. In the case of Sybase database, deadlocks usually occur when the wrong locking scheme is applied on a table. For example, for a table that is used in high volume processing, the locking scheme that locks at a row level instead of locking at a page level or table level would need to be used to avoid deadlocks.

In the case of deadlocks, the usual task for SREs would be to re-run the failed processing that failed due to deadlocks.

Transaction log filling up

RDBMS databases that I have worked with like Sybase and SQL Server have a transaction log for each of the databases in the database server. These transaction logs store the before and/or after rows from the `INSERT/DELETE/UPDATE` commands. When a large transaction is executed, it is possible for this log to be filled up quickly. A common process is to set up regularly and clear this log to a backup store for future analysis if required. Depending on the size of the log and the frequency at which the log is cleared, database rows need to be inserted/deleted/updated in batches. The example in the removing toil chapter to purge database rows uses the batching technique.

End user monitoring

In the current age where the internet is accessible from a mobile device even in remote locations and there is a significant increase in the number of people utilizing online services, certain applications have grown to having millions of users. Users are now using online services across different devices like desktops, mobile phones and tabs, and different browsers across devices with different operating systems. Mobile apps also run on different operating systems. Monitoring, in this case, is not just needed to capture errors occurring on user apps but also to capture the user behaviour.

While SREs require information about any errors or slowness on the user end, product managers/business users require information about which features are being used more, the percentage of users in different locations, usage percentage across devices, and so on.

DNS monitoring

DNS resolution is the first thing that happens for services accessed by external end users. Anything wrong in the DNS resolution will be a major incident as users cannot access the services. DNS monitoring includes checking that the DNS resolution happens correctly and is also performing well. Depending on the number of countries that an organization operates, there might be different top-level domains like .com, .in, .sg, and so on.

While external end users use the public DNS for the routing of their requests, organizations also use internal DNS servers for internal private network. Certain applications/services within an organization are not external facing and are only used within the organization. In such cases, organizations use IP addresses within the network and an internal DNS server which does the DNS resolution within the network. In such cases, SREs also need to monitor if the DNS resolution is correctly happening for internal domain names and also that the resolution is happening quickly.

Monitoring Tools

There are a number of tools out there that can be used for monitoring infrastructure, application, end users, and DNS. There is no one open-source tool that can meet all of the monitoring requirements. However, there are a few vendor tools that meet these requirements as a single solution.

For the purpose of this book, we will consider the open-source tools that can together be used to meet the monitoring needs. The open-source monitoring tools can be seen under a single view in **https:// openapm.io**. At the time of writing this chapter, the list of tools is under **https://openapm.io/landscape**.

The monitoring tools fall under the categories given below. There are also open-source libraries that can be used in application code which will be covered in *Chapter 8: Observability*.

Agents

Agents are used for collecting various types of information. A few examples are as follows:

- CPU, memory, file System, IO, and network metrics information from virtual machines and containers running on Docker host or PaaS platforms like Kubernetes.
- Network level information from packets exchanged between servers. For example, the source and destination IP address and port for a packet.
- Logs of application services and PaaS platform components. For example, error logs written by an application service.
- Time taken to process user requests.
- Metrics from application components like MQs, databases, proxies, and so on.

Transport

After the information is gathered by the agents, some of the agents provide configuration options that can be set up to directly store the collected information into a database. And some of the agents provide an option to stream data to a transport tool like Kafka or rsyslog.

Collectors

Collectors are intermediate tools which collect information gathered by the agents which is further used in sending the collected information to a transport tool or directly to a storage. Some of the collectors like Fluentd provide APIs that can be used to send data to a central Fluentd collector. A Fluentd example will be provided in *Chapter 8*: *Observability*. The Prometheus server is another example which will be explained later in this chapter.

Data transformation

Some of the tools are useful to transform the data gathered by the agents from one format into another format. LogStash is an example of a tool which can be used to convert log lines into JSON format which can then be stored in Elastic Search or can be sent to other output sources like Kafka. LogStash also has other input plugins like receiving data from Kafka. Examples of LogStash will be provided in *Chapter 8*: *Observability*.

Storage

Storage tools help store the information gathered by the Agents directly, transformed by Data Transformers or information gathered by instrumentation libraries like OpenTelemetry. ElasticSearch, MongoDB, InfluxDB, MySQL are a few of the examples to store the monitoring data.

Alerting

Once the data is stored in the databases, alerts can be generated when there are exceptions identified from application logs, high CPU/memory/disk resource utilization on servers or containers, slow responses to lo large number of user requests, and so on. With a vast amount of metrics and log information that is stored into the databases, it is not recommended to check for any issues manually but alerts are set up to automatically identify and send alerts over email, SMS, messaging apps like Slack, pager, and so on. ElastAlert is one such tool and usage examples are provided later in the chapter.

Dashboarding

Visualization/dashboarding tools are used to view the monitoring data in a graphical form or in the form of dashboards. If you are someone who is already working in the IT industry, you might have observed donuts and graphs in different colors that are displayed on large screens in the operations area. These are the dashboards that are used for live status of the services or the infrastructure. While alerts can be set up for specific known problems, the dashboards or visual graphs can be used to keep an eye on the overall health of the application.

The next section gives examples of some of the monitoring tools.

Prometheus

Prometheus is an open-source monitoring tool that was originally developed at SoundCloud. Prometheus can be used to gather information through its supported agents called exporters, instrument application using the Prometheus client libraries, store the gathered information in a time-series database, query the stored information using a query language called PromQL, visualize the data in a graph format in Prometheus UI, and finally, generate alerts using the Prometheus Alert Manager.

When mapped to the above categories of tools, Prometheus components meet the requirements of having an agent, client library, collector, database, visual tool, and alerting.

The Prometheus server gathers/scrapes metrics from what are called targets in the Prometheus terminology. The target can be a virtual machine, container, database or health check end points of applications/services.

Time-series data that is collected by the server from the exporters is a series of data points collected at regular intervals. The default frequency in Prometheus is 60 seconds. For example, when the node exporter of Prometheus is downloaded and run on a Linux Virtual Machine, it is invoked by the server to gather the CPU, memory, and disk information every 60 seconds (or as per the frequency set in the configuration file).

An example of running Prometheus on a Mac system is as follows:

The first step is to download Prometheus and the Node exporter zip files from **https://prometheus.io/**. After they are extracted, the folder would have a file called **prometheus.yml**. This default configuration file in the Prometheus server can be changed to what is mentioned below to extract the Mac OS metrics every 15 seconds. The target in this example is the node exporter that has a default port number of **9100**:

```
global:
  scrape_interval:     15s
  evaluation_interval: 15s

scrape_configs:
- job_name: node
  static_configs:
  - targets: ['localhost:9100']
```

The next step is to start the node exporter from the extracted folder accessed using the terminal or the command line.

```
./node_exporter
```

On starting the exporter, it prints an INFO log line which provides the information that it started successfully. The log line also provides the port number on which the node exporter can be invoked to scrape metrics by the Prometheus server. In this case, the port of the node exporter is the default **9100**:

```
level=info ts=2020-09-06T10:50:53.600Z caller=node_exporter.go:191 msg="Listening on" address=:9100
```

After starting the node exporter, the Prometheus server can be started from the terminal or the command line from the extracted folder. This is shown as follows:

```
./prometheus --config.file=prometheus.yml
```

On starting the server, it provides an INFO log line which provides information that it started successfully and listens on the default **9090** port:

```
level=info ts=2020-09-10T17:17:37.912Z caller=web.go:523 component=web msg="Start listening for connections" address=0.0.0.0:9090
```

It also provides a log line saying that it is ready to accept web requests.

```
level=info ts=2020-09-06T07:30:47.557Z caller=main.go:673 msg="Server is ready to receive web requests."
```

The following are graphical representations in the Prometheus UI for the CPU and memory information that is stored in the Prometheus database:

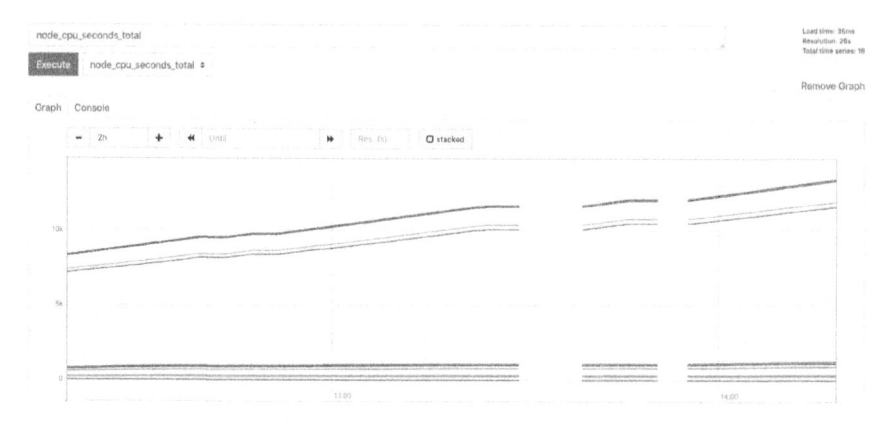

Figure 7.2

The following memory graph shows how the memory utilization varied between 2.8 GB and 3.5 GB in a 2 hour window:

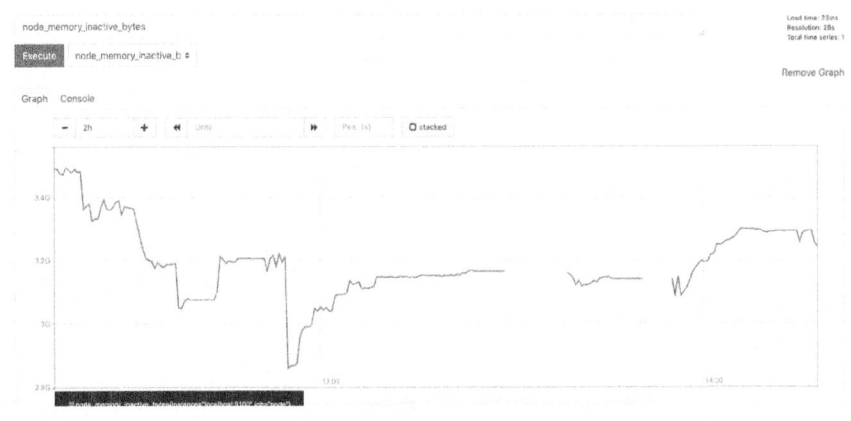

Figure 7.3

Metricbeat

Metricbeat is a tool that can be used to collect a virtual machine, container, and application services metrics. It is one of the Beats in the Elastic Stack. When deployed on a Linux/Windows Virtual Machine or a Mac host, it can collect metrics like CPU, memory, file system, and IO. It also works on Docker hosts and Kubernetes to get the metrics from the containers.

Metricbeat can export the collected metrics to Elastic Search, Logstash, Kafka, Redis, Flat file, or Console.

For our example, we will use elasticsearch as output. The latest versions of Elastic Search and Metricbeat can be downloaded from **https://www.elastic.co/**.

After extracting the downloaded files, ElasticSearch can be started with the following command:

```
./elasticsearch
```

On running the preceding command on the console, certain log lines are written. The following are a few INFO log lines from the output from which we can see that it started on the default port of **9200** and that it is a BASIC open-source version of Elastic Search.

```
[2020-09-10T22:59:26,513][INFO ]
[o.e.h.AbstractHttpServerTransport] [Vishnus-MacBook-Air.
local] publish_address {127.0.0.1:9200}, bound_addresses
{[::1]:9200}, {127.0.0.1:9200}
```

```
[2020-09-10T22:59:26,525][INFO ][o.e.n.Node               ]
[Vishnus-MacBook-Air.local] started]


[2020-09-10T22:59:30,087][INFO ][o.e.l.LicenseService
] [Vishnus-MacBook-Air.local] license [56afb99c-c11d-473a-
b624-09479ef94c9c] mode [basic] - valid
[2020-09-10T22:59:30,090][INFO ]
[o.e.x.s.s.SecurityStatusChangeListener] [Vishnus-MacBook-
Air.local] Active license is now [BASIC]; Security is
disabled
```

Before starting Metricbeat, know that it has various modules for different data to be collected. By default, the system metrics are enabled and the remaining are disabled. This can be seen by running the following command:

```
./metricbeat modules list
```

The command will output a long list of modules with the system metrics enabled by default.

```
Enabled:
system

Disabled:
activemq
aerospike
….
….
….
```

Metricbeat has a configuration file in the YAML format which can be seen in the downloaded and extracted Metricbeat folder. The following is the configuration with which we will start it. The first part of the configuration tells Metricbeat to collect metrics for all enabled modules. The template settings sets the shards for the index to: 1. The output section provides details of Elastic Search running on localhost. The final processors section provides details of additional metadata that can be added to the collected metrics.

```
# =========================== Modules configuration
============================

metricbeat.config.modules:
```

```
  path: ${path.config}/modules.d/*.yml
  reload.enabled: false

setup.template.settings:
  index.number_of_shards: 1
  index.codec: best_compression


# ---------------------------- Elasticsearch Output ------------------------------
output.elasticsearch:
  hosts: ["localhost:9200"]

processors:
  - add_host_metadata: ~
```

Metricbeat can be started with the following command. When started, in our case, it provides INFO logs with its output as Elastic Search and the Elastic Search index template.

```
./metricbeat -e

2020-09-10T23:07:54.390+0530    INFO   [publisher_
pipeline_output] pipeline/output.go:143 Connecting to
backoff(elasticsearch(http://localhost:9200))

2020-09-10T23:07:55.377+0530    INFO   template/load.
go:101 template with name
'metricbeat-7.9.1' loaded.
```

As soon as Metricbeat is started, it will start to collect the metrics. The following URL can be accessed in a browser to look at the indexes created in Elastic Search by Metricbeat. A part of the output is given below which shows the index name and document count at that time. As Elastic Search stores the data in the form of documents.

http://localhost:9200/_cat/indices?v

```
index
docs.count
metricbeat-7.9.1-2020.09.10-000001              309
```

The documents in the index can be looked at in the browser by using the following URL in a browser. We can see that the documents have metrics of CPU, memory, filesystem, process, and so on.

http://localhost:9200/metricbeat-7.9.1-2020.09.10-000001/_doc/_search?q=*

The following is a sample document that has the memory metrics. We can see that approximately 3.1 GB out of 8.5 GB is free.

http://localhost:9200/metricbeat-7.9.1-2020.09.10-000001/_doc/LeUYeXQBihnWpPfFZi5u?pretty

```
"system" : {
  "memory" : {
    "used" : {
      "bytes" : 8556716032,
      "pct" : 0.9961
    },
    "free" : 33218560,
    "actual" : {
      "free" : 3157889024,
      "used" : {
        "bytes" : 5432045568,
        "pct" : 0.6324
      }
    },
    "swap" : {
      "free" : 0,
      "total" : 0,
      "used" : {
        "bytes" : 0,
        "pct" : 0
      }
    },
    "total" : 8589934592
  }
},
```

Grafana

Grafana is a tool that can be used for visualization and alerting from Grafana Labs. It can be used to create dashboards, explore metrics and logs, setting up alerts, and so on. It supports multiple data sources including Graphite, InfluxDB, Prometheus, Elasticsearch, AWS CloudWatch, and more.

For our example, we will use the metrics collected from Metricbeat to create a Dashboard in Grafana.

The first step is to download/install Grafana based on the OS from the installation instructions in **https://grafana.com**.

For Mac, Homebrew can be used to install Grafana using the following brew install command.

brew install grafana

Grafana gets installed in the following directory:

/usr/local/Cellar/grafana/7.1.5/

The default configuration can be looked at in the following directory:

/usr/local/Cellar/grafana/7.1.5/share/grafana/conf/

The default port where Grafana starts up is the port **3000** which can see by the following **grep** command.

grep http_port /usr/local/Cellar/grafana/7.1.5/share/grafana/conf/defaults.ini
http_port = 3000

Grafana can be started using the **brew services** option.

brew services start grafana

Once started, Grafana can be accessed with the following link in the browser. The default username/password are **admin/admin**.

http://localhost:3000/login

120 ■ *Hands-on Site Reliability Engineering*

After logging in, a data source needs to be added from the **Configuration** menu. In our example, we will add the Elastic Search database where the metrics collected by Metricbeat are stored.

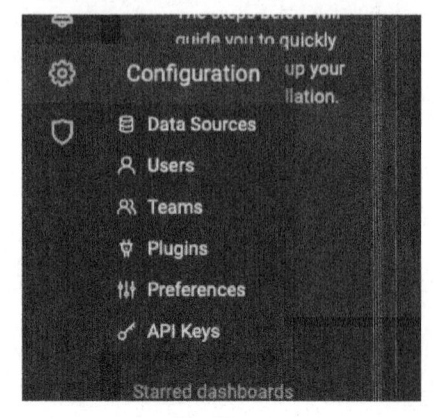

Figure 7.4

The following image shows the Elastic Search URL:

Figure 7.5

The next image is the index to be used in the **Add Data Source** screen for Elasticsearch.

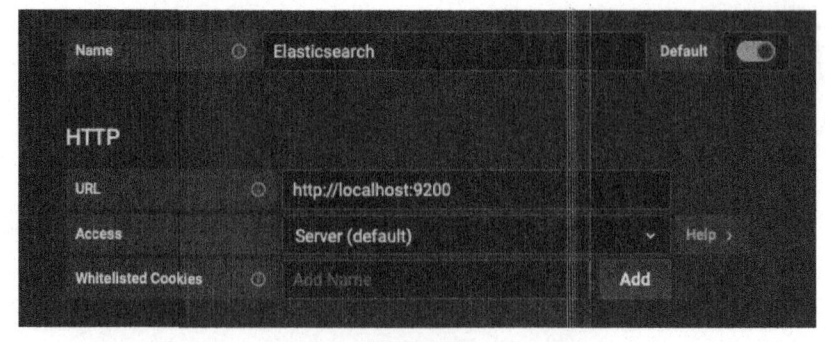

Figure 7.6

After setting up the data source, the dashboard can now be created using the Dashboards menu option. In this example, a simple graph has been added for viewing the system memory metrics. Grafana provides an in-built drop down to choose the last 5 mins, 15 mins, 30 mins, 1 day, 7 days, and so on. The following is the view of the memories captured in the last 15 mins. As we can see, there is a dip in the user memory which was released when the Docker daemon was exited in the system.

The following image also shows the query setup of querying memory metrics and calculating average memory usage for every 10 seconds.

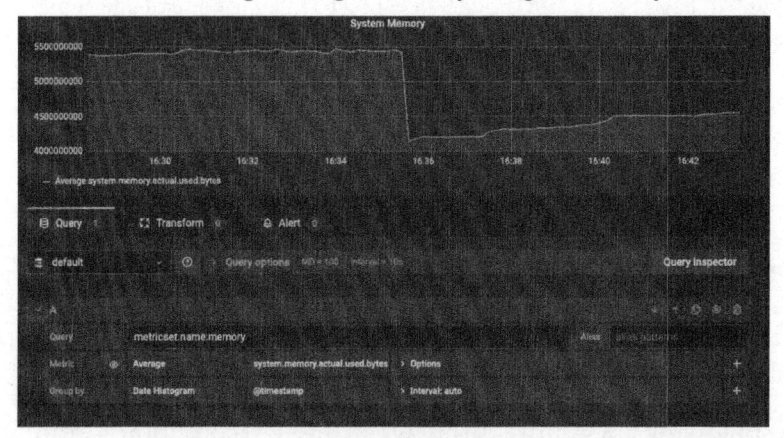

Figure 7.7

Within the created dashboard, Grafana also provides an option to create alerts. Alerts are useful to send notifications immediately when a condition is met. In the following image, we can see an alert that is set up with a condition of memory usage greater than 5 GB for a period of 5 mins. Once an alert condition is met, a notification can be sent through various supported channels like Email, messaging apps like Microsoft Teams, Slack, Telegram, Kafka, and so on. The alerts can also be checked through the Grafana alert API.

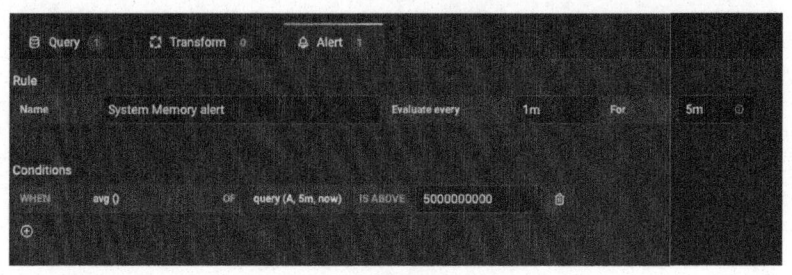

Figure 7.8

The Grafana alert API can be accessed from the **/api/alerts** path.

http://localhost:3000/api/alerts/

The following is a sample output when the created alert is still being evaluated and the alert status is **pending**.

[{"id":1,"dashboardId":2,"dashboardUid":"4uTxwZOGk","dashboardSlug":"system-memory","panelId":2,"name":"System Memory alert","state":"pending","newStateDate":"2020-09-12T18:44:48+05:30","evalDate":"0001-01-01T00:00:00Z","evalData":{"evalMatches":[{"metric":"Average system.memory.actual.used.bytes","tags":{},"value":5353865216}]},"executionError":"","url":"/d/4uTxwZOGk/system-memory"}]

The following is a sample output when the alert condition is evaluated to be true. The status now is **alerting**.

[{"id":1,"dashboardId":2,"dashboardUid":"4uTxwZOGk","dashboardSlug":"system-memory","panelId":2,"name":"System Memory alert","state":"alerting","newStateDate":"2020-09-12T18:49:48+05:30","evalDate":"0001-01-01T00:00:00Z","evalData":{"evalMatches":[{"metric":"Average system.memory.actual.used.bytes","tags":{},"value":5351033750.068966}]},"executionError":"","url":"/d/4uTxwZOGk/system-memory"}]

The following is a sample output when the alert condition is evaluated to be false. The status now is **ok**.

[{"id":1,"dashboardId":2,"dashboardUid":"4uTxwZOGk","dashboardSlug":"system-memory","panelId":2,"name":"System Memory alert","state":"ok","newStateDate":"2020-09-12T19:21:35+05:30","evalDate":"0001-01-01T00:00:00Z","evalData":{},"executionError":"","url":"/d/4uTxwZOGk/system-memory"}]

We have now seen how Grafana can be used to create dashboards from stored metrics with few clicks and configuration. In the future chapter, we will see how Grafana can be used to track the SLIs.

ElastAlert

ElastAlert is a framework that can be used to generate alerts from the data in Elastic Search. It was created at Yelp. ElastAlert details can be looked at their GitHub link: **https://github.com/Yelp/elastalert**.

In our example, we will install ElastAlert and detect a problem using ElastAlert. ElastAlert can be installed using pip. As ElastAlert now supports only Python 3.x, we need to use pip3 to install.

```
pip3 install elastalert --user
```

ElastAlert uses a config file to configure various options. In our example, we will use a simple configuration which tells ElastAlert to check for alerts every one minute, buffer time of 15 minutes, the hostname for ElasticSearch host, port number of ElasticSearch, and finally, how long a failed alert notification is to be re-tried. The following is the content from the **config.yaml** file.

```
run_every:
  minutes: 1

buffer_time:
  minutes: 15

es_host: localhost

es_port: 9200

alert_time_limit:
  days: 1
```

We will also create a rule file for the same example to alert when the memory usage is above 5 GB, which is about 60%. Given below is the content from the **example_single_metric_agg.yml** file. This has details similar to the alert that we have set up in Grafana alert. We are telling ElastAlert to look at the metricbeat index, the metric of user memory and the aggregation to be average. Here, we also provided the document type which happens to be **_doc**.

The min threshold and max threshold are lower and upper bound of expected values. The config given below tells to raise an alert if the used memory is below 30% or greater than 50%.

Finally, we set the alert to be debug and to be printed on the console instead of having external notification options.

```
name: Metricbeat CPU Spike Rule
type: metric_aggregation

index: metricbeat-*
```

```
metric_agg_key: system.memory.actual.used.pct
metric_agg_type: avg
query_key: agent.hostname
doc_type: _doc

bucket_interval:
  minutes: 5

sync_bucket_interval: true

min_threshold: 0.3
max_threshold: 0.6

filter:
- term:
    metricset.name: memory
alert:
- "debug"
```

ElastAlert can be run from the console by giving the rule and config file path. The **--debug** prints the debug messages on console.

```
/Users/vishnu/Library/Python/3.8/bin/elastalert      --debug
--rule   /Users/vishnu/Documents/elastalert-master/example_
rules/example_single_metric_agg.yaml --config /Users/vishnu/
Documents/elastalert-master/config.yaml
```

The following are important messages that we can see on running ElastAlert. The first is that it is starting up; there are no disabled rules and the sleep interval.

```
INFO:elastalert:Starting up
INFO:elastalert:Disabled rules are: []
INFO:elastalert:Sleeping for 59.999892 seconds
```

Next in the log, we can see that it has identified that the threshold condition is met and the alert is found. It also gives the current used percentage as 0.612 while the threshold is 0.5.

```
INFO:elastalert:Alert for Metricbeat CPU Spike Rule,
Vishnus-MacBook-Air.local at 2020-09-12T18:50:00Z:
INFO:elastalert:Metricbeat CPU Spike Rule
```

```
Threshold violation, avg:system.memory.actual.used.pct
0.612 (min: 0.3 max : 0.5)

@timestamp: 2020-09-12T18:50:00Z
agent.hostname: Vishnus-MacBook-Air.local
metric_system.memory.actual.used.pct_avg: 0.612
num_hits: 101
num_matches: 6

INFO:elastalert:Ran Metricbeat CPU Spike Rule from 2020-
09-13 00:00 IST to 2020-09-13 01:00 IST: 0 query hits (0
already seen), 6 matches, 0 alerts sent
```

I modified the rule to set the threshold to 0.8 and re-ran ElastAlert.

```
min_threshold: 0.3
max_threshold: 0.8
```

In this case, we cannot see that the condition is met. Also, we can see no matches found for the given condition.

```
INFO:elastalert:Ran Metricbeat CPU Spike Rule from 2020-
09-13 00:00 IST to 2020-09-13 01:04 IST: 0 query hits (0
already seen), 0 matches, 0 alerts sent
```

Conclusion

While there is merit in monitoring all of the above-covered areas that contribute to running services efficiently, a mistake that many organizations end up doing is implementing siloed monitoring for each of these areas. Also, the multitude of tools in this space which often do not communicate well with each other—adds to the problem of too many alerts getting generated from many systems, which overwhelms the operations teams at times.

In the next chapter, you will learn about how these challenges with a standard way of monitoring which is being streamlined by the practice of observability.

Multiple choice questions

1. The following are the types of Infrastructure monitoring.
   a) Server monitoring
   b) Network monitoring
   c) Storage monitoring
   d) All of the above

2. The following are steps to achieve proper monitoring.
   a) Logs/metrics collection
   b) Storage
   c) Alerting
   d) All of the above

3. Following are monitored as part of container monitoring.
   a) Container metrics
   b) Service logs
   c) Only a
   d) Both a and b

Answers

1. d
2. d
3. d

CHAPTER 8
Observability

One of the most common challenges with monitoring is the amount of noise that it creates which makes it difficult to understand the real issues from the false alarms. The primary reason for this stems from the fact that monitoring is typically applied as an isolated, disconnected system which monitors a component of a service as an individual entity, and not as a piece of a larger ecosystem with dependencies and integrations affecting one another. This ends up being a system which at the most is best at stating 'what' is broken in a service at a symptomatic level, without really stating what might have caused it or led to that situation.

Observability is a term borrowed from the world of control theory which is defined as the ability of a system to provide insights of its internal state based on how its exterior is behaving. When applying this to IT, it means that observability is a property associated with an application, rather than an implementation on the application and its associated components.

Structure

In this chapter, we will discuss the following topics:

- Goals of observability
- Three pillars of observability
- Open source libraries and tools

Objective

Right from the end-user accessing an application in a browser or mobile application and all the way to the application code running on an on-premise/PaaS/IaaS platform, a request goes through a number of hops and it is important to capture the end to end flow to both measure key metrics and analyze any failures. Observability is a gradual evolution of monitoring which is becoming popular as application architectures are evolving from monolith to microservices which involves multiple services coming together to provide an end user service.

This chapter will provide insights into how to make an application more observable and will also give examples from open source tools to achieve full-stack observability.

Goals of observability

Building observability for a system should never be treated as a goal in itself. There needs to be clarity on the areas of improvement that observability is targeting. This helps in ensuring that observability is aligned with the expectations of the stakeholders and is also customized to the organization's specific needs. Some of the key areas which are targeted by observability are as follows:

Service reliability

Observability provides insights into a service like the performance of the service relative to the pre-defined baseline. The metrics could be providing details on the key areas of availability and latency of the service. Observable services are able to provide proactive alerts when a system is either deviating or is about to deviate from the expected path on these two key areas. Getting notified on this deviation at the earliest enables the application support teams to take corrective actions to either completely eliminate or reduce the impact to the service.

Operational efficiency

Along with improvements in the areas of **mean time to recover (MTTR)** and **mean time to detect (MTTD)** which we discussed in the previous chapters, observability also directly impacts another important area which is now being termed as the **MTTI** or **mean time to investigate**.

MTTI is defined as the time taken by an organization to start investigating the cause and the path for solving the issue since the issue was detected. The insights enabled by observability can shorten this period by pinpointing the cause upfront and helping the team get on with resolving the issue at the earliest.

As the observable system emits the right signals at the right time and has the warning signals built in, they enable the operations teams to efficiently spend their time and avoid focusing on irrelevant areas. This helps improve the operational efficiency of the organization.

As an example, imagine a scenario where an application has 80% of its user base from a specific region like the south east of Asia which is indicated through the monitoring set on the traffic flow attribute of the networking components. The monitoring systems may be contributing to making the observable by alerting any major decrease in the traffic from the South East Asian region and routing the traffic through a different region, say Europe. A service which has mature observability baked in will be able to perform a few checks on the different hops to determine if a failure in a particular node in the route has caused this shift in trend or if this is in fact a genuine change in user the behavior. In case of the former scenario, the necessary alert needs to be generated whereas in case the latter is true, there is no need for an alarm.

Security and compliance

By providing a 360-degree view of a service's state which is achieved by corelating logs from multiple systems like applications, integration points, network and hosting infrastructure; an observable system is able to provide critical insights into the security and compliance requirements of a system. With correlation between network patterns, data usage, and access logs, certain security behavior of the system can be analyzed and alarms can be triggered for any anomalies.

Any organization that wants to achieve high standards of security should start thinking about observability with focus on security. Having a **SIEM** (**security information and event management**) which is able to aggregate, corelate, and notify on security anomalies helps organizations monitor user and system behaviors related to security.

Three pillars of observability

The three pillars of observability are as follows:

- Metrics
- Logs
- Traces

In the previous chapter, we looked at different types of logs and metrics. While logs and metrics are useful and suitable for monitoring monolith applications or applications with small number of components/services, these do not completely capture all the data required to monitor applications with a large number of micro-services. In the previous chapter, there is a mention of modern applications that are used across different devices such as desktops, mobile phones, and tabs and different browsers across devices with different operating systems. A single user action from a user can pass through a number of services in the background. For example, a simple buy transaction on a mobile app of an ecommerce company can involve some or many of the following services. All the services by themselves can run on different platforms, are written in different programming languages, have their own databases, and integrate with external services for payments.

- Login service
- Customer service
- Product service
- Vendor service
- Location service

- Inventory service
- Order service
- Pricing service
- Promotion service
- Payment service
- Recommendation service

In these kinds of architectures of micro-service applications, there is additional data which is needed, that is, the data of the services that have a request from the user passed through, the time that each hop in the request took, the start time and end time of each hop, and if there is a failure, the hop in which the failure occurred. This is the third piece of data and this is referred to as tracing, or more specifically, distributed tracing for distributed processing. While distributed tracing has been there for a few years now, it has gained wider popularity with the evolution of the mobile internet and the increased number of users for online services. More and more companies are breaking their traditional monoliths into micro-services and startups are building the applications as micro-services right from the start.

Some important components of tracing are as follows:

Standardized libraries/APIs/SDKs

With distributed tracing becoming a very common need these days, there are standardized APIs/SDKs available that can be used to achieve the required trace information. OpenTracing and OpenCensus are two such standards that are in use. These two standards have now combined and a new standard called OpenTelemetry has been formed. Telemetry is about collecting and exporting data that is required for monitoring, hence the name OpenTelemetry is very suitable. OpenTelemetry is in the Beta version and the API and SDKs are available for the most-used programming languages. And there are collectors and exporters to different destinations to store the trace data like Prometheus, Jaeger, Zipkin, and so on. The latest status can be checked at **https://opentelemetry.io**. In the next section of the chapter, we will see an example of OpenTelemetry for Python.

Standardized trace context

Trace context is the information that is included in a trace to identify the end to end lifecycle of a trace across applications. While using OpenTelemetry, each trace contains multiple spans (hops in the entire journey of the request). Each span carries a context to uniquely identify itself and to relate to the parent span and the main trace identifier.

The W3C trace context is an upcoming standard to include standardized trace information in HTTP headers. When the trace information is used in the headers, it helps achieve some amount of tracing even when one of the service in the entire flow isn't instrumented and also when different applications involved in a trace use different tools.

Tracers

Tracers are store the trace information. Some example of tracers are Jaeger, Zipkin, Prometheus, Elastic APM, and so on.

Cardinality attributes

Cardinality attributes are additional attributes that are added to the tracing info to differentiate one trace from the other for use in analysis when there are errors in processing, or when there are performance issues, or any other issues that may occur. These attributes can be business specific information like customer id, transaction id, payment type, and so on. or some technical information like the device of the originating request, the OS/platform on which a service is running, location detail, the related node/pod ID, and so on.

This information can be useful in identifying what caused the problem while the trace itself helps provide info on where the problem occurred.

Open source libraries and tools

In the previous chapter, an introduction has been given to OpenAPM and examples of some of the agents and collectors, and storage, dashboarding, and alerting tools for infrastructure monitoring. In this chapter, we will focus on the frameworks, libraries, shippers/

transporters and transformers for application logs and traces. The storage, dashboarding, and alerting tools will be similar tools whether it is for infra or application monitoring data.

Filebeat

Filebeat is one of the Elastic beats (the previous chapter introduced Metricbeat). Filebeat is used to collect and forward log messages. Filebeat can be configured to receive input from different sources like log files, AWS Cloudwatch, Kafka, exposing an HTTP endpoint for Filebeat, and so on. For the purpose of our example, we will look at logs picked from a log file.

When installed on a virtual machine, it can start monitoring multiple log files and forward/ship to a specified output. It has various features, for example, to only read a specific pattern of lines and not all the lines. So, a use case example can be to read only the ERROR log messages and not the INFO ones.

In terms of the output, Filebeat can send collected logs directly to ElasticSearch or to other tools in data pipeline like Logstash, Kafka, and so on. The Filebeat output can also be load balanced by sending log lines to different Elasticsearch instances or Logstash instances as an example to handle any high volume and split the load to different output instances.

Filebeat can be set up by different ways as mentioned in the Elastic site. At the time of writing this book, the downloaded version was 7.9 and it is available in documentation in the following link:

https://www.elastic.co/guide/en/beats/filebeat/current/index.html

On a Mac laptop, this will just download and unpack the downloaded file with the following two commands:

```
curl -L -O https://artifacts.elastic.co/downloads/beats/filebeat/filebeat-7.9.2-darwin-x86_64.tar.gz
tar xzvf filebeat-7.9.2-darwin-x86_64.tar.gz
```

After unpacking, the Filebeat will need to be configured. The folder structure will be as follows:

```
Vishnus-MacBook-Air:filebeat-7.9.2-darwin-x86_64 vishnu$ ls -ltr
total 240352
```

```
-rw-r--r--    1 vishnu   staff       13675 Sep 23  2020 LICENSE.txt
-rw-r--r--    1 vishnu   staff     8440372 Sep 23  2020 NOTICE.txt
-rw-r--r--    1 vishnu   staff      114090 Sep 23  2020 filebeat.reference.yml
-rw-r--r--    1 vishnu   staff     2402200 Sep 23  2020 fields.yml
-rw-r--r--    1 vishnu   staff         809 Sep 23  2020 README.md
-rwxr-xr-x    1 vishnu   staff   112073136 Sep 23  2020 filebeat
drwxr-xr-x    3 vishnu   staff          96 Sep 26 22:39 logs
drwxr-xr-x   59 vishnu   staff        1888 Sep 26 22:40 modules.d
drwxr-xr-x   60 vishnu   staff        1920 Sep 26 22:40 module
drwxr-xr-x    3 vishnu   staff          96 Sep 26 22:40 kibana
-rw-------    1 vishnu   staff         252 Sep 27 01:02 filebeat.yml
drwxr-xr-x    5 vishnu   staff         160 Sep 27 12:28 data
```

In our example, we will configure Filebeat to read the lines from a log file. The sample log file is given below. The configuration tells Filebeat to read lines from the file booktest.log as they are written, pick only the lines which start with the word **ERROR**, add an additional field by the name **extrafield** value of **extrafieldvalue** and store collected logs in Elasticsearch. The **extrafield** here is an additional field that can be added to the output if there is a need to add any specific identification field for this log to be later searched in Elasticsearch.

```
filebeat.inputs:
- type: log
  enabled: true
  paths:
    - /Users/vishnu/Documents/booktest.log
  include_lines: ['^ERROR']
  fields:
     extrafield: extrafieldvalue


# --------------------------- Elasticsearch Output ------------------------
output.elasticsearch:
  # Array of hosts to connect to.
```

```
hosts: ["localhost:9200"]
```

After configuring, Filebeat can be started with below command.

```
./filebeat -e
```

The following are some important INFO log lines that provide information that the process has started and it logs metrics every 30 seconds and there is a mention of the starting of the harvester for the log file. The sample metrics output will be provided as an example after we write some lines to the log file.

```
2020-09-26T23:25:26.040+0530    INFO    [monitoring] log/log.go:118    Starting metrics logging every 30s
2020-09-26T23:25:26.040+0530    INFO    instance/beat.go:450 filebeat start running.
2020-09-26T23:25:26.058+0530    INFO    log/harvester.go:299 Harvester started for file: /Users/vishnu/Documents/booktest.log
```

Below is a sample Python file which writes 10 **ERROR** and 9 **INFO** logs to the file that we configured with Filebeat.

```
testfile=open('booktest.log', 'w')
for i in range(0,10):
        testfile.write('ERROR: Test Message Number ' + str(i) + '\n')

for i in range(11,20):
        testfile.write('INFO: Test Message Number ' + str(i) + '\n')

testfile.close()
```

On running the preceding script, we can see that the metric given below in the Filebeat output logs where it states 19 events were read from the file and only 10 events that matched the **include_lines** condition have been acknowledged in the output. These are the 10 **ERROR** log messages that were written to the log.

```
2020-09-26T23:27:56.086+0530    INFO    [monitoring] log/log.go:145    Non-zero metrics in the last 30s    {"monitoring": {"metrics": {"beat":{"cpu":{"system":{"ticks":401,"time":{"ms":6}}, "total":{"ticks":1942,"time":{"ms":10}, "value":1942},"user":{"ticks":1541,"time":
```

```
{"ms":4}}},"info":{"ephemeral_id":"b8560ea9-2cf8-467a-
9c07-f07e6e08fdf8", "uptime":{"ms":150336}},"memstats"
: {"gc_next":56557680,"memory_alloc":48949224,
"memory_total":205208136,"rss":-2195456},"runtime":
{"goroutines":26}}, "filebeat":{"events":{"active":-
19,"done":19}, "harvester":{"files":{"a04182b9- edfa-
4d0f- 8f4e-81b3026415dc":{"size":551}} ,"open_
files":1,"running":1}},"libbeat" :{"config": {"module":
{"running":0}},"output":{"events": {"acked":10,
"active":-10}}, "pipeline":{"clients":1,"events":
{"active":0},"queue":{"acked":10}}},"registrar":
{"states":{"current":1,"update":19},"writes":
{"success":1,"total":1}}
,"system":{"load":{"1":3.4561,"15":3.6353,"5":3.5469,
"norm" :{"1":0.864,"15":0.9088,"5":0.8867}}}}}}
```

The shipped log lines can be viewed from the browser on the created Filebeat index.

http://localhost:9200/filebeat-7.9.2-2020.09.26-000001/_search?q=*

If we have look at a single document from the Elastic index, we can do a get it with the below sample link in the browser based on the _id values in the link mentioned precedingly. In the Elastic document, we can see the actual message, the additional field we added, and the host on which the Filebeat was running.

http://localhost:9200/filebeat-7.9.2-2020.09.26-000001/_doc/ BQePy3QB0-HEBymL_Cpu?pretty

```
{
  "_index" : "filebeat-7.9.2-2020.09.26-000001",
  "_type" : "_doc",
  "_id" : "BQePy3QB0-HEBymL_Cpu",
  "_version" : 1,
  "_seq_no" : 0,
  "_primary_term" : 1,
  "found" : true,
  "_source" : {
    "@timestamp" : "2020-09-26T17:57:21.119Z",
    "message" : "ERROR: Test Message Number 0",
    "input" : {
      "type" : "log"
    },
```

```
    "fields" : {
      "extrafield" : "extrafieldvalue"
    },
    "agent" : {
      "type" : "filebeat",
      "version" : "7.9.2",
      "hostname" : "Vishnus-MacBook-Air.local",
      "ephemeral_id" : "b8560ea9-2cf8-467a-9c07-f07e6e08fdf8",
      "id" : "98faf329-5558-46f8-9c72-6ddc1136576e",
      "name" : "Vishnus-MacBook-Air.local"
    },
    "ecs" : {
      "version" : "1.5.0"
    },
    "host" : {
      "name" : "Vishnus-MacBook-Air.local"
    },
    "log" : {
      "offset" : 0,
      "file" : {
        "path" : "/Users/vishnu/Documents/booktest.log"
      }
    }
  }
}
```

Logstash

Logstash is another tool from Elastic Stack that can ingest data from different sources, transform them, and send the transformed data to a configured output. Input sources can be Filebeat, RabbitMQ, Kafka, Twitter streaming API, syslog, and so on. or it can receive the events by exposing a HTTP endpoint.

The output of Logstash can be Elasticsearch, Graphite, MongoDB, Kafka instance, Zabbix, and so on.

Logstash supports various filters to process the data either to transform the received data into a more structured format, drop the received data based on a certain condition, perform some processing using ruby code, and so on. In the example in this book, we will look at the grok filter which can be used to transform the data to a more structured format.

There are various ways to set up Logstash based on the platform and the chosen method. At the time of writing this book, the Logstash documentation is available at the following link:

https://www.elastic.co/logstash

The **logstash** folder will look as follows on extracting.

```
Vishnus-MacBook-Air:logstash-7.9.2 vishnu$ ls -ltr
total 1272
-rw-r--r--@   1 vishnu   staff    601073 Sep 23  2020 NOTICE.TXT
-rw-r--r--@   1 vishnu   staff      2276 Sep 23  2020 CONTRIBUTORS
-rw-r--r--@   1 vishnu   staff     13675 Sep 23  2020 LICENSE.txt
-rw-r--r--@   1 vishnu   staff      4041 Sep 23  2020 Gemfile
-rw-r--r--@   1 vishnu   staff     22951 Sep 23  2020 Gemfile.lock
drwxr-xr-x    5 vishnu   staff       160 Sep 27 01:10 logstash-core-plugin-api
drwxr-xr-x   22 vishnu   staff       704 Sep 27 01:17 bin
drwxr-xr-x    6 vishnu   staff       192 Sep 27 01:19 lib
drwxr-xr-x    5 vishnu   staff       160 Sep 27 12:28 logs
drwxr-xr-x    6 vishnu   staff       192 Sep 27 12:28 data
drwxr-xr-x    8 vishnu   staff       256 Sep 27 12:28 config
drwxr-xr-x   14 vishnu   staff       448 Oct 22 22:57 x-pack
drwxr-xr-x    5 vishnu   staff       160 Oct 22 22:57 modules
drwxr-xr-x    3 vishnu   staff        96 Oct 22 22:57 tools
drwxr-xr-x    4 vishnu   staff       128 Oct 23 12:23 vendor
drwxr-xr-x    6 vishnu   staff       192 Oct 23 12:23 logstash-core
```

In order to understand the transformation by Logstash using the grok filter, we will change our log line in the Python script to include some additional information – the timestamp of the log message, the script name, and the line number.

```
from datetime import datetime

testfile=open('booktest.log', 'w')
for i in range(0,10):
```

```
        testfile.write("ERROR: " + datetime.now().
strftime('%Y-%m-%d %H:%M:%S.%f%z') + "|log_generator|3|Test
Message Number " +  str(i) + "\n")

for i in range(11,20):
        testfile.write('INFO: Test Message Number ' +  str(i)
+ '\n')

testfile.close()
```

Logstash instance uses a configuration file. The following is the sample configuration that we use in our example. We are using a grok filter that parses the input lines collected by Logstash and the output is sent to the booktest-logs index in Elasticsearch.

```
input {
  beats {
    port => 5044
  }
}

filter {
  grok {
    match => { "message" => "% {WORD:error_level}: %{TIMESTAMP_ISO8601: timestamp_match}\|%{WORD:source}\|%{NUMBER:linenum}\|%{GREEDYDATA:log_message}" }
  }
}

output {
  elasticsearch {
    hosts => ["http://localhost:9200"]
    index => "booktest-logs-%{+YYYY.MM.dd}"
  }
}
```

The configuration of Filebeat is also changed in this example to send the output to Logstash instead of sending the output directly to Logstash.

```
filebeat.inputs:
- type: log
```

```
    enabled: true
    paths:
      - /Users/vishnu/Documents/booktest.log
    include_lines: ['^ERROR']

# ----------------------------- Logstash Output ---------
----------------------
output.logstash:
    hosts: ["localhost:5044"]
```

The next step after the preceding changes is to restart Filebeat and start Logstash.

./filebeat -e

./logstash -f ../config/logstash-sample.conf

After Filebeat and Logstash are running, the following Python command can be executed to generate the content again.

python log_generator.py

After the log content is generated again using the generator script, we can see the index creation in Elasticsearch and look for documents in the Index.

http://localhost:9200/booktest-logs-2020.09.26/_search?q=*

One of the documents from the above link can be used to check the details in the document. We can see that Logstash has transformed the individual log message into multiple fields like **log_message**, source, linenum, and timestamp instead of storing the log line as it is in the Elasticsearch database. This is a simple example of how transformation works. In the real world for SREs, there might be different types of logs and in different formats to transform. The transformation helps in building dashboards later in tools like Grafana or generating alerts based on this transformed data that is stored in Elasticsearch. For example, depending on the service name or source file that causes an error, the alert may need to be sent to different teams.

http://localhost:9200/booktest-logs-2020.09.26/_doc/mAf4y3QB0-HEBymLZypq?pretty

{
  "_index" : "booktest-logs-2020.09.26",

```
  "_type" : "_doc",
  "_id" : "mAf4y3QB0-HEBymLZypq",
  "_version" : 1,
  "_seq_no" : 3,
  "_primary_term" : 1,
  "found" : true,
  "_source" : {
    "tags" : [
      "beats_input_codec_plain_applied"
    ],
    "linenum" : "3",
    "source" : "log_generator",
    "@timestamp" : "2020-09-26T19:51:26.306Z",
    "input" : {
      "type" : "log"
    },
    "message" : "ERROR: 2020-09-27 01:21:24.838630|log_generator|3|Test Message Number 0",
    "@version" : "1",
    "timestamp_match" : "2020-09-27 01:21:24.838630",
    "log_message" : "Test Message Number 0",
    "ecs" : {
      "version" : "1.5.0"
    },
    "host" : {
      "name" : "Vishnus-MacBook-Air.local"
    },
    "log" : {
      "file" : {
        "path" : "/Users/vishnu/Documents/booktest.log"
      },
      "offset" : 0
    },
    "agent" : {
      "version" : "7.9.2",
      "hostname" : "Vishnus-MacBook-Air.local",
      "type" : "filebeat",
      "name" : "Vishnus-MacBook-Air.local",
      "ephemeral_id" : "992e7051-c10a-42d8-bdd8-08c6b07c1e35",
      "id" : "98faf329-5558-46f8-9c72-6ddc1136576e"
```

```
        },
        "error_level" : "ERROR"
    }
}
```

Fluentd

Fluentd is another option to choose from as a data collector. It can collect data from various sources and transform the data and send to a configured output. Fluentd can receive application logs of various languages, syslog, Kafka, AWS Cloudwatch, and so on. The output of Fluentd can be Elasticsearch, AWS S3, Kafka, RabbitMQ, MySQL, Zabbix, Slack, and so on. Further information on various input and output options for Fluentd can be looked at the Fluentd site **https://www.fluentd.org/**.

To understand how Fluentd works with an example, we will look at the same log file example, grok and print the output on the console.

To set up Fluentd, the pre-requisite is to install ruby and bundler.

On MacOS, these can be installed with the following commands:

```
brew install ruby
sudo gem install bundler
export PATH="/usr/local/opt/ruby/bin:$PATH"
```

After installing ruby and bundler, the next is to install Fluentd. There are multiple ways of installing/setting up Fluentd. I chose the option to set it up from source by cloning the **git** repo and running the following commands.

```
git clone https://github.com/fluent/fluentd.git
cd fluentd

bundle install
bundle exec rake build
gem install pkg/fluentd-1.11.2.gem

cd bin
./fluentd --setup ./fluent
```

After setting up Fluentd with above commands, the next is to set up the grok plugin which does not come by default. The grok plugin can be downloaded from the **git** repo. The **.rb** files will be available in the **/lib/fluent/plugin/** folder of the downloaded repo. These need to be copied to the same **/lib/fluent/plugin/** folder path where Fluentd is set up above.

https://github.com/fluent/fluent-plugin-grok-parser

Fluentd also uses configuration files like other tools. There are various input plugins and we are using the **tail** plugin here to read the latest lines written into a file. The file pointer is maintained by Fluentd in the **pos_file**. The same grok filter used in the above Logstash example is used here.

```
## File input
<source>
  @type tail
  path /Users/vishnu/Documents/booktest.log
  pos_file /Users/vishnu/Documents/booktest.log.pos
  tag book.test
  <parse>
    @type grok
    <grok>
      pattern %{WORD:error_level}: %{TIMESTAMP_ISO8601:timestamp_match}\|%{WORD:source}\|%{NUMBER:linenum}\|%{GREEDYDATA:log_message}
    </grok>
  </parse>
</source>

## match tag=book.test and print to console
<match book.test>
  @type stdout
</match>
```

After creating the configuration file, Fluentd can be started with the following command.

```
./fluentd -c ./fluent/fluent_booktest.conf -vv &
```

Given below are important info messages that can be looked at when Fluentd is started. We can see the logs details from the configuration file on the file being read, the tail and grok plugins being used, and the expansion of the used Grok filter.

```
2020-09-27 17:07:13 +0530 [info]: fluent/log.rb:329: info:
starting fluentd-1.11.2 pid=4057 ruby="2.7.1"

2020-09-27 17:07:14 +0530 [info]: fluent/log.rb:329:info:
adding match pattern="book.test" type="stdout"
2020-09-27 17:07:14 +0530 [info]: fluent/log.rb:329:info:
adding source type="tail"

2020-09-27 17:07:14 +0530 [trace]: #0 fluent/log.rb:
286:trace: registered parser plugin 'grok'

2020-09-27 17:07:14 +0530 [info]: #0 fluent/ log.
rb:329:info: Expanded the pattern %{WORD:error_
level}: % {TIMESTAMP_ISO8601:timestamp_
match}\|%{WORD:source}\|%{NUMBER:linenum}\|%
{GREEDYDATA:log_message} into (?<error_level>\b\
w+\b): (? <timestamp_match>(?:(?>\d\d){1,2})-
(?:(?:0?[1-9]|1[0-2]))-(?:(?:(?:0[1-9])|(?:[12]
[0-9])| (?:3[01])|[1-9]))[T ](?:(?:2[0123]|[01]?[0-
9])):?(?:(?:[0-5][0-9])) (?::?(?:(?:(?:[0-5]?[0-9]|60)
(?:[:.,][0-9]+)?)))?(?:(?:Z|[+-](?:(?:2[0123]| [01]?[0-
9]))(?::?(?:(?:[0-5][0-9])))))?)\|(?<source>\b\w+\
b)\|(?<linenum> (?:(?:(?<![0-9.+-])(?>[+-]?(?:(?:[0-
9]+(?:\.[0-9]+)?)|(?:\.[0-9]+))))))\| (?<log_message>.*)

2020-09-27 17:07:14 +0530 [debug]: #0 fluent/log.rb:308:
debug: tailing paths: target = /Users/vishnu/Documents/
booktest.log | existing =
2020-09-27 17:07:14 +0530 [info]: #0 fluent/log.rb:329:
info: following tail of /Users/vishnu/Documents/booktest.
log
2020-09-27 17:07:14 +0530 [info]: #0 fluent/log.rb:329:
info: fluentd worker is now running worker=0
```

After Fluentd is started, the booktest.log can be written with the same Python script.

`python log_generator.py`

The output after parsing can be seen in the console where Fluend was started.

```
2020-09-27 17:07:37.496847000 +0530 book.
test: {"error_level":"ERROR","timestamp_
match":"2020-09-27 17:07:37.381916","source":"log_
```

```
generator","linenum":"3","log_message":"Test Message 
Number 0"}
2020-09-27 17:07:37.496918000 +0530 book.
test: {"error_level":"ERROR","timestamp_
match":"2020-09-27 17:07:37.386639","source":"log_
generator","linenum":"3","log_message":"Test Message 
Number 1"}
```

Fluentd has another input plugin called the forward. The forward plugin allows sending messages to the Fluentd instance as the programs get executed. An example can be seen below.

The configuration file for this example is shown below where there is the type of forward used and two sets of matches based on the input being sent to Fluentd from a sample Python script.

```
<source>
  @type forward
  port 24224
</source>

<match book.test.errorlogs>
  @type stdout
</match>

<match book.test.infologs>
  @type stdout
</match>
```

Fluentd forward requires a Python package to be installed for Python. There is a different requirement for other programming languages. For Python, this can be installed using **pip**.

```
pip install fluent-logger
```

The following is the sample script that forwards log messages to a running Fluentd instance. It is to be noted that log data needs to be sent in JSON format.

```
from fluent import sender
from fluent import event
from datetime import datetime
sender.setup('book.test', host='localhost', port=24224)
event.Event('errorlogs', {"logtype": "ERROR", "logtime": 
datetime.now().strftime('%Y-%m-%d %H:%M:%S.%f%z'),
```

```
"source": "log_generator", "linum": 5, "message":
"Exception XYZ occured"})
event.Event('errorlogs', {"logtype": "INFO", "logtime":
datetime.now().strftime('%Y-%m-%d %H:%M:%S.%f%z'),
"source": "log_generator", "linum": 6, "message":
"Transaction 1234 processed"})
```

On running the preceding script, we can see these JSONs printed in the Fluentd console.

```
2020-09-27 18:22:41.000000000 +0530 book.test.errorlogs:
{"logtype":"ERROR","linum":5,"message":"Exception
XYZ occured","logtime":"2020-09-27
18:22:41.400520","source":"log_generator"}
2020-09-27 18:22:41.000000000 +0530 book.test.errorlogs:
{"logtype":"INFO","linum":6,"message":"Transaction
1234 processed","logtime":"2020-09-27
18:22:41.404799","source":"log_generator"}
```

OpenTelemetry

At the beginning of this chapter, OpenTelemetry was introduced. Here, we will take a look at an example of using OpenTelemetry for a Flask application. The following Python packages will need to be installed and using pip3 as we need to use Python 3.x for this example.

```
pip3 install opentelemetry-api
```

```
pip3 install opentelemetry-sdk
```

```
pip3 install opentelemetry-instrumentation-flask
```

```
pip3 install opentelemetry-instrumentation-requests
```

Given below are two small flask apps that will be used in this example. The first app calls the second one and the second one has a 5 second delay added to visibly see that the span for the second app took more time in the entire trace.

Save this flask app as opentelemetry_example.py. This app uses the libraries installed using pip3 and sets the tracer as console so that the output is printed to the console.

```
import flask
import requests
```

```
from opentelemetry import trace
from opentelemetry.instrumentation.flask import
FlaskInstrumentor
from opentelemetry.instrumentation.requests import
RequestsInstrumentor
from opentelemetry.sdk.trace import TracerProvider
from opentelemetry.sdk.trace.export import (
    ConsoleSpanExporter,
    SimpleExportSpanProcessor,
)

trace.set_tracer_provider(TracerProvider())
trace.get_tracer_provider().add_span_processor(
    SimpleExportSpanProcessor(ConsoleSpanExporter())
)

app = flask.Flask(__name__)
FlaskInstrumentor().instrument_app(app)
RequestsInstrumentor().instrument()

@app.route("/")
def flasktraceex():
    tracer = trace.get_tracer(__name__)
    with tracer.start_as_current_span("flask-example"):
        requests.get("http://localhost:5001")

    return "Done, view the trace on the console"

app.run(debug=True, port=5000)
```

Save this flask app as **opentelemetry_example_12.py**. In this, **time.sleep(5)** adds a 5 second delay to the response.

```
import flask
import time

app = flask.Flask(__name__)

@app.route("/")
def flasktraceex12():
      time.sleep(5)
      return "Done, held this for 5 seconds"
```

```
app.run(debug=True, port=5001)
```

After creating the files, the next step is to start the two flask apps.
```
python3 opentelemetry_example.py
python3 opentelemetry_example_12.py
```

Open a browser and access the first app running on port **5000**.

http://localhost:5000

After about 5 seconds, the trace output can be seen on the console. There are three spans here. The first to be seen on the console is the last hop which is the call to the second app. The context information mentioned earlier in the chapter about trace id, span id, and linking the span to its parent span can be seen in this example. For each span, the start time, the end time, and the status codes are also output to the console. From the start time and end time of these three spans, it can be observed that the most time-consuming part of the original request were the 5 seconds taken by the second app. This way, the span causing problems can be identified in true production as well with real applications. As status codes are also part of trace information, the errored spans can also be looked at.

We have put the output to console but in real production, tracers are used to store the spans and the traces are also visualized in dashboard and can be alerted using alerting tools.

Span 3
```
    "name": "HTTP GET",
    "context": {
        "trace_id": "0x5c190d68dcb1fd6e71c8956d061db8f8",
        "span_id": "0xd7c35b9a56bd1766",
        "trace_state": "{}"
    },
   "parent_id": "0x764480008198fd9b",
    "start_time": "2020-09-27T18:23:37.846504Z",
    "end_time": "2020-09-27T18:23:42.862545Z",
        "http.url": "http://localhost:5001",
        "http.status_code": 200,
```

Span 2
```
    "name": "flask-example",
    "context": {
        "trace_id": "0x5c190d68dcb1fd6e71c8956d061db8f8",
        "span_id": "0x764480008198fd9b",
        "trace_state": "{}"
    },
    "parent_id": "0x706f45007a64afb1",
    "start_time": "2020-09-27T18:23:37.846362Z",
    "end_time": "2020-09-27T18:23:42.863219Z",
```

Span 1
```
    "name": "flasktraceex",
    "context": {
        "trace_id": "0x5c190d68dcb1fd6e71c8956d061db8f8",
        "span_id": "0x706f45007a64afb1",
        "trace_state": "{}"
    },

    "parent_id": null,
    "start_time": "2020-09-27T18:23:37.845593Z",
    "end_time": "2020-09-27T18:23:42.863975Z",
```

Conclusion

As a concept, observability is still relatively new. As different organizations start adopting it, there are many improvements that can be done. It is important to understand that observability has been introduced to simplify a support team's work and this needs to be always kept in mind while building observable systems. It is easy to over engineer and build a complex framework for observability which further adds to the woes of the development and support teams, and this completely beats the purpose.

Building observable systems is a journey and it is necessary that inputs from multiple stakeholders are taken into consideration along the way.

At this juncture in the book, many important topics on SRE have been covered which has prepared you as a reader for the next chapter which will explain some of the most critical areas of site reliability engineering like error budgets, SLIs, and SLOs.

Multiple Choice Questions

1. Which of the following is not a part of the three pillars of observability?
   a) Logs
   b) Metrics
   c) Alerts
   d) Traces

2. Which of the following pillars have gained more popularity with more and more use of micro-services architecture?
   a) Logs
   b) Metrics
   c) Traces
   d) None of the above

3. Which of the following is/are component(s) of distributed tracing?
   a) APIs/SDKs
   b) Trace context
   c) Tracers
   d) All of the above

Answers

1. c
2. c
3. d

CHAPTER 9
Key SRE KPIs: SLAs, SLOs, SLIs, and Error Budgets

In most cases, an application's effectiveness can be attributed to its ability to keep its users happy and wanting to come back. An application which is unstable, slow to respond, or intermittently unavailable can be a big put off for its users which can result in its low utilization. Therefore, it becomes important that the overall quality of the service offered to the external users is measured continuously. This not only helps in understanding the current state of the user experience but also can throw light on what the key areas are that need to be improved for the applications or service.

Structure

In this chapter, we will discuss the following topics:

- Key metrics for SRE
- Service level objectives (SLOs)
- Service level indicators (SLIs)
- Service level agreements (SLAs)
- Error budgets

Objective

In order to understand how a service is actually performing, you will have to devise accurate and creative ways to measure the performance of the service. But this task might be easier said than done unless you have spent considerable time and effort on building a strategy to measure your service performance and followed it through with effective implementation. In this chapter, you will learn how to measure the quality of the service being offered to the end users and the ways to ensure that the level of the services being offered is above a certain quality standard.

One of the key principles on which site reliability is built is accepting that failures are normal. Also, SREs understand that getting to 100% availability is very costly and might not really be possible as the ecosystem which uses the applications will have multiple components and factors outside the control of the SREs that will have availability less than 100%. This chapter will also cover techniques used by SREs to pick the relevant baselines for measuring an application's service quality.

Key metrics for SRE

SREs ensure that failures occurring in any component of the application's ecosystem are not impacting its users to an extent that is starts hurting the business. It is important that the failures are contained within the boundaries of what can be considered as acceptable behavior of the application. In order to define what is acceptable, there is a need to develop an understanding on what are the expectations of a user from the application and how effectively the organization can convert those into metrics that can be baselined and continuously measured.

The above requirement can be met by defining certain SRE relevant for the application. While measuring these metrics is not the end goal and will not address the issues associated with an application, it helps in narrowing down as to what could be causing the service to fall below the expected or acceptable standards. This eventually leads towards identifying the areas of improvement that should be focused by the application support teams.

The SRE practice has evolved towards four keys measurements which are compared against a baseline defined for each. These four measurements are as follows:

- **Service level objectives** or **SLOs**
- **Service level indicators** or **SLIs**
- **Service level agreements** or **SLAs**
- Error budgets

SREs manage the service quality of an application, including any failures by using SLOs, SLIs, error budgets, and error budget policies.

Service level indicator (SLI)

Earlier in the introductory chapter of SRE, we learnt briefly that **service level indicator** (**SLI**) is a measure of how a service is performing at a given point in time. In this chapter, we will look at what those measurements are and which of those are applicable for different types of applications.

The well-known terms when it comes to what to measure are the four golden signals, measuring based on the USE method and the RED method. The four golden signals as mentioned in the Google SRE book are latency, traffic, errors, and saturation.

The USE method refers to three things to measure for a given resource. The resource for servers/VMs can be disk, CPU, memory, network, and so on.

- **Utilization**: Utilization refers to the amount that a resource is being utilized.
- **Saturation**: Saturation refers to the point at which a resource gets saturated.
- **Errors**: Error refers to the number of error events.

The RED method refers to three things to measure for microservices which are as follows:

- **Rate**: The number of requests that are received.
- **Errors**: The number of requests that error out.
- **Duration**: The amount of time to process a request.

As a person who has worked on database centric applications of a part of my career, I can relate the RED method to both databases and microservices. We can just replace "requests" with "queries or stored procedure calls."

While there are different methods that provide guidelines of what needs to be measured, it is important for the SRE team to check what is suitable for the production system that they are maintaining.

For example, for an ecommerce website/mobile app or any other consumer application (payments, social media, and so on), the most important thing to remain competitive in terms of user experience is the speed of processing and an extremely low number of errors. The end to end processing should be done within milli seconds (less than a second) and the number of errors might be as low as 1 in a 1000.

For a high frequency trading or algorithmic trading applications, the amount of time to read a change in stock price and the amount of time that the buy/sell transaction is sent back to exchange needs to be extremely low. Certain financial companies go to the extent of co-locating their infrastructure or infrastructure which is in close proximity with the exchange to reduce the latency caused by the network. The accuracy of the decided transaction should also be very high to avoid loss from the buy/sell transaction.

For regulatory reporting applications, there are two types of applications. The first is the batch based where the end of day reports are generated and sent to regulators. The second type are real time reporting applications. For these applications, again, the accuracy and timely reporting plays a key role to avoid penalties on wrong reporting. Whether the reporting happens during the end of the day or in near real time, accuracy is the key. For timeliness, certain regulators put the requirement as "as soon as technically possible." In such cases, companies need to do it in the best possible way to report.

In this end to end flow of these three examples, there can be multiple applications or microservices that will be involved. Considering the duration of the end to end flow will be a sum of the time taken across all applications/services; each hop will have to complete its processing in much lesser time than the overall time. Similarly, different applications/services will need to maintain higher quality of their data and processing logic to avoid any errors.

As it is being repeatedly mentioned in different chapters, these days, consumers accessing a website or mobile app can do it from different browsers and devices with each device running a different operating system. While measuring errors, it is not just about measuring those in the backend services, but the measurement should also be done in the front end applications to help in the analysis of errors. After all, for an end user, whether the error occurs in the front end or the backend, it is still an error. For example, all errors related a particular OS or a particular browser, and so on. An efficient **end user monitoring (EUM)** helps in this case.

In terms of the actual measurement of the SLIs, whether it is the request processing rate/throughput, error rate, processing time of requests, quality of data, queue depth for message queues, and so on, the actual techniques to carry out the measurement have been introduced in the two previous chapters on monitoring and observability. Any of the OpenAPM tools or a combination of them or a vendor solution can be used to measure the SLIs. For example, a Grafana dashboard can be created for the purpose of looking at SLI. The dashboard by itself can read from Elasticsearch or Prometheus.

Service Level Objective (SLO)

Service level objective (SLO) is the target level for an SLI. For example, if the SLO is that the availability percentage of the service should be 99%, then the SLI of availability should be greater than or equal to 99%. For example, an SLI can be 99.1%, 99.5%, and so on.

An SLO of 99% availability means that the maximum downtime that is possible for the service is 3.65 days per year.

If the SLO for the service is that the number of requests that get serviced greater than one second are 1000, then the SLI of number of slow requests should be less than or equal to 1000.

You might be wondering why we need to mention an SLO of 99% and why we can't have 100% for an availability target. While this may sound good theoretically, it is very difficult because of various practical reasons to maintain that level of availability. For every 9 that gets added into the availability target, the more difficult it gets to meet that need. For example, 99%, 99.9%, 99.99%, and so on. There should be a real revenue difference to the business to ask for an extra 9 in the availability. For example, what the revenue loss is if the availability is 99% vs 99.9% and comparing it with the cost it takes in the infrastructure and other quality aspects of the application/ service to get to a level of that extra 9. In one of the future chapters, we will look at different techniques of how to reach higher levels of availability and that chapter will also provide an insight into the extra cost that gets associated as more and more techniques are utilized to improve the availability percentage. For example, setting up a load balancer and four instances of a service running across four different VMs or four different replicas/containers requires an availability of additional infrastructure.

A similar cost requirement will exist for other SLOs like higher quality of processing data, faster processing of requests, and so on.

Note that SLOs are measured based on a time period such as one week or two weeks. Later in the chapter, we will look at the concept of error budget and error budget policies that provide information on the consequences of SLO breach.

Service level agreement (SLA)

An SLA is a more generic term than the other measurements of SRE and has existed much before the practice of SRE came into fray. An SLA is an agreement between the provider of the service and the consumer of the service and is often captured in a legal contract between these two parties. When the service provider and consumer organizations are different, the impact of an SLA getting breached is usually set as a financial penalty, although it could be in any other form that the two organizations have decided. In certain cases, especially in a B2C kind of service where a consumer might not be directly paying for the service, a formal SLA is not defined. But this does not mean that a poor-quality service will not be detrimental to the organization. It will have a brand and reputation impact for the service provider and will eventually impact the service provider.

Typically, SREs are not involved in defining the SLA which is driven by business and the customer facing teams. The SRE team's contribution to defining an SLA is often limited to providing the SLO as inputs to the teams defining the SLA. An SLA is usually defined more loosely than an SLO, and as long as the organization is able to meet its SLO, the SLA should be met as well.

It is important that meeting an SLA is not just motivated by saving the financial penalties for the organization. It should be treated as a means of improving the quality of service that is being offered to the consumers.

An SLA should have the following attributes of a service covered:

- **Service**: The service that is being measured.
- **Severity level**: The extent of impact of the service attribute (critical, important, info).
- **Details/description**: Information on the attribute which will help the users understand what exactly is being measure.
- **Target SLA**: The specific target for the service.
- **Metric**: The attribute of the service that is being measured. For example, availability, performance, and so on.

Error budgets

In the previous chapter, we learnt that error budget, as the name suggests, is the "budget" that can be used up for "errors," technically a missed SLO. We also learnt that SREs accept failure as normal and they maintain the production service in a way that the SLOs are met and calculated risks are taken to experiment if the current SLI is much better than the agreed SLO. For example, an experiment to upgrade to a new version of the OS on some of the servers can be done when the error budget is not exhausted. Once it is successful, the same can be applied to further servers. Or the frequency of releases can be increased when the error budget is not exhausted.

Similarly, any improvements to the application/service based on the tech backlog/debt can be picked up and experimented when there is a sufficient error budget. This helps clear the technical debt while also meeting the expectations of the business users or the end customers of the application/service.

In scrum teams, it is important for the scrum team, PO, and scrum master to encourage the tech backlog stories to be also picked up in the Sprints to clear those and keep reducing the possibility of an error budget exhausting in the future. For example, the application/service processing time might be impacted due to a higher volume of users which might be expected in the future. Given the opportunity to improve the performance of the application through tech backlog stories, for example, with a 10-20% of allocation of tech backlog tasks in the overall sprint backlog, the application/service will be ready for the future.

While these points are on what can be done when the SLIs are better than the SLOs, there are also cases where the SLIs are poor than the target SLOs, that is, the error budget is exhausted.

Error budget policy

SREs maintain a documented error budget policy which states what can be done when the SLOs are met and what can/cannot be done when the SLOs are being missed. For example, the error budget policy might state that all releases are to be halted (other than emergency fixes) until a root cause analysis and resolution of source issue causing frequent miss of SLOs is completed. Missed SLOs lead to analysis and finally user stories for the design and development/ scrum teams to complete before actual the feature releases. Any technical improvements to fix the issues causing the errors go into the tech backlog/debt of the application.

To avoid any issues in the future, it is recommended that the SLOs and error budget policies are set up right at the beginning of starting the development for a new application.

For any existing applications/services, it might be challenging to explain to users what the SLOs/error budget policies are and why they are required. It may be helpful if the users are also taken through awareness sessions on the importance of SRE and these concepts of SRE.

Conclusion

Defining the different service level metrics and error budget can seem like a daunting task in the beginning. It is important to understand that getting these values right might take a few iterations and you will get better at defining them with practice. Also, in many cases, these values will not remain static but will evolve with changes in the busines and internal changes within the organization. Reviewing the relevance of the metrics periodically is a good practice and is recommended.

With the baselines in place, a natural next step is to focus on areas of improvement in the applications service quality. This is required to ensure that the quality of service meets the defined thresholds. Chaos engineering and automation testing are examples of two such areas. The next chapter will provide a detailed explanation on these areas.

Multiple choice questions

1. The following is a not a term coined as part of SRE evolutions.
   a) SLA
   b) SLI
   c) SLO
   d) Error budget

2. For an availability target of 99.9%, the error budget of downtime possibility in minutes per week is:
   a) 10
   b) 100
   c) 1008
   d) None of the above

3. Which of the following can be a possible mention in an error budget policy?
   a) Penalizing dev team for exhaustion
   b) Penalizing SRE team for exhaustion
   c) Stopping major releases
   d) None of the above

Answers

1. a
2. a
3. c

Chapter 10
Chaos Engineering

The modern application development teams have numerous technological choices for the application components (programming languages, databases, MQs, cache, load balancer, proxy, gateway, sidecars, and so on), infrastructure (on-premise, cloud, PaaS platforms) and the way that deployments are done. Each team makes a choice from the available options based on their need. For example, an application which expects low volume that can be handled by a single instance can chose to deploy on an EC2 instance or an on-premise VM directly. Another application that expects a large number of requests and also varying volume in different periods can choose to deploy their services on Kubernetes with auto-scaling enabled so that the number of containers can be increased and decreased based on the traffic.

In a large organization, a user request from a mobile/web app or end of the day backend processing involves interactions between many of these applications that are built and deployed differently. Within a single application itself, the modern applications involve multiple micro-services that can again be built and deployed differently. With continuous technological advancements, the complexity is only growing. With the growing complexity, combined with the need to do frequent releases of incremental deliveries, there arises a question to question how confident we are in our applications/services, the infrastructure, and the interactions of these applications with other applications. There are numerous unknowns. The following are a few examples of these unknowns in certain conditions:

- User interfaces that may crash
- Annoying errors to users
- Unhandled exceptions
- Gaps in observability data
- Missed out alerting rules from monitoring
- Missed out scenarios for auto-recovery

Given these unknowns, there is a need to improve the confidence in our systems. This chapter introduces the chaos engineering practice that helps in finding answers to these questions and improving the confidence in our systems. Multiple companies have adopted the chaos engineering practice and the adoption is only growing.

Structure

In this chapter, we will discuss the following topics:

- Introducing chaos engineering
- Chaos engineering process
- Chaos GameDays
- Injecting failures
- Techniques to improve resiliency of an application/service

Objective

By the end of this chapter, the reader will be able to understand the need for chaos engineering and the different types of failure conditions. You will understand the process of conducting chaos experiments. You can get hands-on with a few chaos experiments and understand a few techniques to improve application resiliency.

Introducing chaos engineering

Chaos engineering is a practice that has evolved in Netflix and the Chaos Monkey tool was created in 2011. The chaos engineer role was created in 2014. On the site **https://principlesofchaos.org**, chaos engineering is defined as follows:

"Chaos engineering is the discipline of experimenting on a system in order to build confidence in the system's capability to withstand turbulent conditions in production."

If you look at the preceding statement, there are three important parts:

- The first is about experimentation. We conduct Chaos experiments to uncover systemic weaknesses. If there are any weaknesses, they will be exposed. Depending on the criticality/severity of the uncovered problem, it can be prioritized and remediated accordingly.
- The second is about building confidence. If the Chaos experiment does not result in any observations/findings, it builds confidence that the system was able to withstand the condition created in the experiment.
- Finally, it's about the turbulent conditions themselves. These are the failure conditions that can occur in production. A Chaos experiment includes simulating these conditions by injecting failures into the system.

The next section explains some of the known conditions that can occur in production.

Application/service unavailability

An application/service can go down in production. It might be that the application/service crashed or it may have been brought down for some maintenance or releases. Whatever the reason may be that this condition occurs, we can observe some of the following by purposefully bringing down an application/service:

- Distribution of production traffic to available instances based on the high availability setup.

- Behavior in UI if certain backend services are completely not available.
- Impact on interfacing applications/services.
- Configuration of the pods in Kubernetes if they are set to auto-scale.
- Verification of alert configuration.
- Automated election of one of the available slaves as master if the master is brought down in a master/slave setup.

Network delays

However much we talk about high-speed networks, there may still be a situation where there is slowness or latency. This may occur as we still have places where there is low speed network and an end user may be in that location. There may also be other reasons that will lead to a latency in the network. In such cases, how does the user interface or a calling service behave?

Also, the latency-related issues can occur inside a company network as well where data centers may be in different locations or due to any other reason.

We can observe some of the following by purposefully injecting this latency condition into the infrastructure:

- Timeout settings
- Handling of re-try storms.
- For example, if a user re-tries a payment/money transfer transaction after the request is already received in the backend, how does the UI handle this to avoid duplicate transfer?
- If the latency is breaching the target in the SLO, is it getting captured in the error budget?

Network failures

While network delay is a situation that can happen in production, there can be failures as well like packet loss, packet corruption, and packet duplication. Again, these can occur in both external and internal networks. The above-mentioned observations can also be applied to a packet loss situation by purposefully dropping outgoing or incoming packets since a loss means that a request might not be back with a response or a request might not even reach the desired target application.

Resource unavailability

Applications use resources like CPU, memory and disk. Whether an application/service is deployed on a VM or a container, there can still be limits on these resources unless vertical scaling is enabled. For example, PCF provides an option to scale vertically for resources in addition to the option of scaling horizontally in terms of the number of instances. The free resources available for use by the application processes/containers can be taken away and the behavior of the application can be observed.

- Out of memory errors
- Write failures when disk is full
- Monitoring and alerting setup to detect this problem

Configuration errors

Every application needs different types of configurations right from the application functionality, drop down values, connection details to other applications, and so on. There are also configurations related to deployment such as configuration of whether scaling is enabled or not, configuration in load balancer, proxy, and so on. A small issue in an important configuration can send an application for toss. Configurations can be corrupted to see how the application is behaving and how quickly we are able to detect that there is a problem in the configuration.

Database failures

There can be different types of failures for databases. And some of these never occur in non-production environments and pop up in production. These are as follows:

- The database process itself might go down. In such a case, is there a high availability setup for the database using the master/slave mechanism?

- Processes might lock one or more tables and block other processes that have to wait for the lock to be released. In such a case, is there a way to identify and kill the offending process?
- Transaction log fill ups occur when large DML transactions are executed and the transaction log that records the before/after records gets filled up quickly. In such a case, it is important to see if there is a recovery that was possible without a database restart.

Database applications are also processed by themselves and need resources like CPU, memory, disk, and so on. Chaos experiments to reduce the available resources can be run against databases as well.

Chaos engineering process

Chaos engineering is about running the chaos experiments. There are a few steps involved in the process of performing chaos experiments.

Define steady state

Firstly, define the steady state of the application. The steady state, for example, can be that "UI will have timeout handling and retry attempts of transaction will be handled."

Build a hypothesis

The next step is to build a hypothesis that the steady state will continue to hold true during the experiment. For example, "When there is packet loss in the network, the steady state will continue to hold true."

To elaborate the scenario here, the request from the UI will reach the backend service and will be processed successfully by the service or a number of services involved in that transaction. However, the response from the service will be dropped and will not go back to the UI. In this case, the UI will receive a timeout but the actual transaction will be completed in the backend.

Minimize blast radius

The next step is to ensure that the chaos experiment is not conducted across the entire infrastructure or services but only on a controlled set. For example, if there are three instances of the backend service is running across three VMs, one of the VMs can be selected to introduce the failure. So, the blast radius in this case will be that one instance.

Inject the failure condition

After the target is selected, an outgoing network loss of, for example, 5% can be applied on the target VM if it is being done in production. A higher percentage value can be used if it is being done in non-production.

The reason for choosing the outgoing direction is to allow the request to reach the VM but drop the response.

Verify hypothesis

After the failure is injected, verify that the hypothesis holds true. Verify the results from dummy transactions or verify the end user monitoring logs.

Certain organizations conduct chaos experiments in production and certain companies conduct in a non-production environment. So, either a test can be conducted in non-production for generating traffic or real user traffic in production can be impacted to see the real impact.

While chaos principles suggest running the chaos experiments in production, certain organizations may choose an approach of doing those in non-production first before running those in production.

Reverse failure condition

After a particular time, either after completion of the tests or a random time, the failure condition should be reversed to put things back to normal. In the next section, we will take a look at how a network delay condition can be injected into a VM and reversed.

Fix any issues

From the verification, it can turn out that everything worked as expected and the hypothesis was true. However, if there were any issues identified from the experiment, the same will need to be analyzed and fixed.

Automate to run continuously

To understand the chaos engineering steps, one scenario was taken and explained above. However, when chaos experiments are run in production, hundreds of scenarios can be considered and automated to run at regular intervals. Fixing any issues will be outside of the experiment. Automated alerting can be set up when the hypothesis in the chaos experiment is not met when the failure is injected.

Chaos GameDays

In certain organizations, Chaos GameDays are conducted on specific planned days. On a GameDay, a number of people including the SREs, chaos engineers, and any other participants are required to get together and they purposefully inject a variety of failures into the infrastructure and applications. Once the failures are injected, they observe if everything is working as expected.

If everything works perfectly with the infrastructure and the application services are resilient to the failures, then that builds a great bit of confidence.

If there are any issues that arise and need to be urgently fixed, the usual incident management processes will be followed and the required remediation will be done. This will also ensure that the SREs know what needs to happen when such a situation occurs during an unplanned time.

A long-term solution for the issues that arise can be taken back to the development teams. The solution may be something that needs to be fixed at an architecture level or at a code level.

Chaos GameDays will involve planning ahead of the day in terms of a number of things:

- Which infrastructure is being targeted?

- Is it about bringing down an entire region and testing failovers or load balancing to other regions?
- Which applications are hosted in it?
- Which SREs need to be involved?
- What failures are to be injected?

Injecting failures

One of the key parts of the chaos experiment is to inject failures and reverse the injected failures wherever possible. It may not always be possible to automatically reverse an injected failure condition, but most failure conditions can be reversed.

In the order of inject failures, there are various open source tools that can be used. The following are some of the examples:

- **Chaos Mesh**: Chaos Mesh can be used to perform chaos experiments on Kubernetes environments.
- **Cthulhu**: Cthulhu is an open source tool that can be used to perform Chaos experiments on AWS, GCP, and Kubernetes. It is also integrated with Slack for notifications on Slack.
- **chaoskube**: chaoskube can be used for Chaos experimentation on Kubernetes. It randomly kills pods in a Kubernetes cluster.
- **Mangle by VMware**: Mangle is an open source software from VMware to run chaos experiments. It provides support for running chaos experiments on Kubernetes, Docker, vCenter, and virtual machines.
- **ChaosBlade by Alibaba**: ChaosBlade is an open source tool from Alibaba to run the chaos experiments. It can be used to run experiments for system resources, JVM, and C++ applications. It also supports running chaos experiments on Docker containers and Kubernetes.
- **Spring Boot Chaos Monkey**: Spring Boot Chaos Monkey can be used to randomly inject failures in Spring Boot applications. The controls of what failures are needed can be configured in the pom file as an example.
- **ChaoSlingr**: ChaoSlingr is an open source tool for security chaos testing. It is used for conducting security chaos testing on AWS.

- **Resiliency Studio by AT&T**: AT&T Resiliency Studio is a self-service resilience validation platform. It can be used to conduct chaos experiments and also comes with an easy-to-use UI.

- **Muxy**: Muxy is a proxy that can be used to simulate real world failures at layers 4, 5, and 7. Muxy can work as an HTTP proxy, TCP proxy, middleware, or can be used as a network shaper.

- **Chaos HTTP Proxy**: Chaos HTTP proxy is an open source proxy that can be used for injecting failures into HTTP requests. Random failures can be sent back on HTTP requests by using this as a proxy while making requests.

- **Sitespeed.io Throttle**: Throttle can be used for simulating different conditions on Mac and Linux. It uses `pfctl` on Mac and `tc` on Linux.

Chaos experiments can be conducted by running a set of commands as well. Though this will not be efficient to configure and perform at scale or run them repeatedly, we will look at these basic commands to understand how failures can be injected.

Killing a process

A running process can be killed with the kill -9 command. The kill -9 or the kill - SIGKILL command kills the process immediately irrespective of what it is doing. The reason for using this is that this might be a real time scenario that can occur in production. Without the -9 option, the default will be the SIGTERM which will tell the process to kill itself gracefully.

Network failures

Different open source tools provide different options to achieve network failures. They mostly fall into the following three options to inject the network failures on a Linux VM:

- The first option is the open source tool which is used by making it a proxy in between the client and the service. It can also be used where one service is calling another service using a proxy. The network failures will be configured in the proxy. Toxiproxy and Muxy are a couple of examples with this proxy option.

- The second option the open source tool uses are the Linux **Traffic Controller (TC) Network Emulator (NetEm)** feature. Network emulation can be used for simulating latency, loss, duplication, and corruption. The **tc** commands can be used to configure the network interfaces to simulate these network scenarios on outgoing packets. For example, the configuration can be done on an ethernet interface.

- The third option is the open source tool uses is iptables. iptables can be used to configure the IP packet filter rules in Linux.

In case of MacOS, the first option given above of using a proxy can be used. Alternatively, Packet Filter (PF) features in MacOS can also be used to inject network failures. **pfctl**, **dnctl**, and **dummynet** binaries are used in MacOS to achieve this.

Linux/Netem

We will look at how Netem can be used to modify configuration on ethernet device on a GCP VM.

The first step is to check the current configuration using the show option of tc command. In my instance, the IP address is mapped to ens4 interface. We can see the right interface, in my case ens4, by using the ifconfig command. Here is the command to display current tc configuration on the ens4 interface.

```
root@hello-gcp-1:/home/vishnu_vardhan_chikoti# tc qdisc show dev ens4
qdisc mq 0: root
qdisc pfifo_fast 0: parent :2 bands 3 priomap  1 2 2 2 1 2 0 0 1 1 1 1 1 1 1
qdisc pfifo_fast 0: parent :1 bands 3 priomap  1 2 2 2 1 2 0 0 1 1 1 1 1 1 1
```

The next is a simple command to inject a delay of 2 seconds on outgoing packets on the interface **eth0** interface.

```
tc qdisc add dev ens4 root netem delay 2000ms
```

After running the above command, the modified setting can be seen by running the show command again. We can see that the 2 second delay is now configured. When this configuration is active, any packets going out of ens4 will have a delay of 2 seconds applied.

```
root@hello-gcp-1:/home/vishnu_vardhan_chikoti# tc qdisc show dev ens4
qdisc netem 8001: root refcnt 3 limit 1000 delay 2.0s
```

To reverse this network failure that was injected, the following command needs to be run to delete the added rule and everything will come back to normal:

```
tc qdisc del dev ens4 root
```

The show command can be run again to see that the configuration is back to what it was before injecting the failure.

```
root@hello-gcp-1:/home/vishnu_vardhan_chikoti# tc qdisc show dev ens4
qdisc mq 0: root
qdisc pfifo_fast 0: parent :2 bands 3 priomap 1 2 2 2 1 2 0 0 1 1 1 1 1 1 1
qdisc pfifo_fast 0: parent :1 bands 3 priomap 1 2 2 2 1 2 0 0 1 1 1 1 1 1 1
```

MacOS/PF

We will now look at how to inject network delay on MacOS by using pfctl, dnctl, and dummynet.

The first step is to enable packet filter (**pf**) by using the following command:

```
Vishnus-MacBook-Air:~ vishnu$ sudo pfctl -E
No ALTQ support in kernel
ALTQ related functions disabled
pf enabled
Token : 11167424444304600893
```

The second step is to create a pipe and call it pipe 1 as an example. This command sets a 1000 ms delay on the packets being routed through this pipe.

```
sudo dnctl pipe 1 config delay 1000
```

The third step is to route all outgoing packets to pipe 1 which was created above. There are multiple options here like routing packets of a specific protocol or routing packets to a specific destination, and so on. For this example, we will simply set all outgoing packets to be routed to pipe 1.

```
echo "dummynet out all pipe 1" |sudo pfctl -f -
```

After completing the setup to add the network delay, we access a website with the time curl option to do the curl and also print the time. We can see that the time taken with the delay configured is about 6 seconds.

```
Vishnus-MacBook-Air:~ vishnu$ time curl -v https://www.xfgeek.com
<Other output>
real    0m5.745s
user    0m0.021s
sys     0m0.025s
```

The configured network delay can be reversed by running the following commands:

```
sudo pfctl -f /and so on/pf.conf
sudo dnctl -q flush
sudo pfctl -d
```

On running the final command above, we can see that the packet filter (**pf**) is now disabled.

```
Vishnus-MacBook-Air:~ vishnu$ sudo pfctl -d
No ALTQ support in kernel
ALTQ related functions disabled
pf disabled
```

After reversing the failure condition, we can access the website again and see that the response time is much faster, about 1 second.

```
Vishnus-MacBook-Air:~ vishnu$ time curl -v https://www.xfgeek.com
<Other output>
real    0m1.262s
```

```
user    0m0.022s
sys     0m0.010s
```

Muxy

We will look at an example of how Muxy can be used as a proxy and a 2 second delay can be achieved.

Muxy can be installed by using the following command:

```
go get github.com/mefellows/muxy
```

By default, the **muxy** binary will be installed in the user's home directory. The following is the location where it is installed on a MacOS:

```
Vishnus-MacBook-Air:bin vishnu$ pwd
/Users/vishnu/go/bin
Vishnus-MacBook-Air:bin vishnu$ ls -ltr
total 23072
-rwxr-xr-x  1 vishnu  staff  11810972 Mar 28 23:47 muxy
```

After installing Muxy, we will start the flask app that was created and used within the blue-green deployment example in the earlier chapter.

```
python flask_docker_example.py
 * Serving Flask app "flask_docker_example" (lazy loading)
 * Environment: production
   WARNING: This is a development server. Do not use it in a production deployment.
   Use a production WSGI server instead.
 * Debug mode: off
 * Running on http://0.0.0.0:5000/ (Press CTRL+C to quit)
```

Next, we will create the configuration file for Muxy. The following is the configuration file. It includes the host and port details of where the Flask app is running and the delay that needs to be applied on requests and responses. A 1 second delay on request and 1 second delay on response makes it a total of 2 seconds delay overall.

```
proxy:
```

```yaml
- name: http_proxy
  config:
    host: 0.0.0.0
    port: 8181
    proxy_host: 0.0.0.0
    proxy_port: 5000

middleware:
  - name: http_tamperer
    config:
      request:
        host: "0.0.0.0:5000"

  - name: delay
    config:
      request_delay: 1000
      response_delay: 1000
```

We then start Muxy using the configuration file mentioned above.

```
Vishnus-MacBook-Air:Documents vishnu$ ~/go/bin/muxy proxy
--config ./muxy_config.yml
2021/03/29 19:20:40.401591 [INFO]        Loading
plugin      http_tamperer
2021/03/29 19:20:40.401610 [INFO]        Loading
plugin      delay
2021/03/29 19:20:40.401676 [INFO]        Loading proxy
http_proxy
2021/03/29 19:20:40.401685 [DEBUG]       HTTP Tamperer
Setup()
2021/03/29 19:20:40.401688 [DEBUG]       Delay Symptom
- Setup()
2021/03/29 19:20:40.402445 [INFO]        HTTP proxy
listening on http://0.0.0.0:8181
```

On doing a curl to the Flask app via the Muxy proxy, we can see that the time taken is more than 2 seconds. For simplicity, only the time section from the curl output is shown here. The other output is removed.

```
Vishnus-MacBook-Air:Documents vishnu$ time curl -v -H"Host: 0.0.0.0:5000" http://localhost:8181/
<Other output>
real    0m2.043s
user    0m0.006s
sys     0m0.012s
```

On doing a curl to the Flask app directly, the response time is very less. It can be seen as follows. Again, only the time section from the curl output is shown here. The other output is removed.

```
Vishnus-MacBook-Air:Documents vishnu$ time curl -v http://localhost:5000/
<Other output>
real    0m0.025s
user    0m0.008s
sys     0m0.009s
```

HTTP failures

Chaos HTTP proxy can be used to inject HTTP failures. The jar file of the proxy can be downloaded from GitHub or the source code can be downloaded and built from the source. For the example here, I directly downloaded the jar file which works on Linux or MacOS.

Chaos HTTP proxy works based on a configuration where the type of HTTP failures and the percentage can be configured. The following is the example configuration that we will use which mentions that the proxy should return 500 errors 10% of the times, 504 errors 10% of the times ,and 80% of the requests should be successful:

```
Vishnus-MacBook-Air:Downloads vishnu$ cat chaos-http-proxy.conf
com.bouncestorage.chaoshttpproxy.http_500=10
com.bouncestorage.chaoshttpproxy.http_504=10
com.bouncestorage.chaoshttpproxy.success=80
```

Once the configuration file is created, the jar file can be started with the configuration file as follows:

```
Vishnus-MacBook-Air:Downloads vishnu$ java -jar chaos-
http-proxy --properties chaos-http-proxy.conf
I 11-21 20:46:10.632 main org.eclipse.jetty.util.log:186
|::] Logging initialized @596ms
I 11-21 20:46:10.677 main o.eclipse.jetty.server.Server:327
|::] jetty-9.2.z-SNAPSHOT
I 11-21 20:46:10.738 main o.e.j.server.ServerConnector:266
|::] Started ServerConnector@673d1dc{HTTP/1.1}
{127.0.0.1:1080}
I 11-21 20:46:10.739 main o.eclipse.jetty.server.Server:379
|::] Started @707ms
```

After starting the jar file, requests can be made through the proxy and we can see a mix of failure and success responses. As an example, I started the Flask app that we used in the earlier chapter where the blue/green deployment example was demonstrated.

Multiple requests can be made to the Flask app to see a mix of failure and success responses.

Random failure response from multiple requests:

```
Vishnus-MacBook-Air:blue vishnu$ curl --fail --proxy
http://localhost:1080 http://localhost:5000
curl: (22) The requested URL returned error: 504 Gateway
Timeout
```

Successful response:

```
Vishnus-MacBook-Air:blue vishnu$ curl --fail --proxy
http://localhost:1080 http://localhost:5000
<!DOCTYPE html>
<html lang="en">
<head>
    <meta charset="UTF-8">
    <title>The blue app</title>
</head>
<body>
```

```
        <h1> Hello Blue ! </h1>
</body>
</html>
```

It is to be noted that since Java is very strict in terms of security, Chaos HTTP proxy cannot by default be used for testing or with websites with https connections. Changes will need to be done by adding certs and re-building.

Injecting multiple failures

It is important to remember that during Chaos experimentation, we inject one failure at a time to the identified weakness and relate it to a cause. If we bring down an instance, inject network latency elsewhere, block resources all at the same time, it will be complete chaos and it might not be possible to narrow down to the cause of the issue that is uncovered.

Techniques for building resiliency

There are a number of things that can be done so that the applications/services handle faults. We will look at some of those here.

Single point of failures

The first thing to do is to avoid single point of failures. The single point of failures can be at different levels. A high availability setup can be done to avoid the single point of failures.

Datacenter

This is the worst that can happen—that the entire datacenter or that particular region goes down or is not available. There can be many reasons for that. Having the infrastructure spread across different datacenters or regions will avoid this problem.

One option in this case is to load balance across regions with active instances across regions. Load balancers by itself can be layer 4 or layer 7 load balancers. That is, load balancers that work at a network level or at an application level.

A network level load balancer is used to distribute traffic to the multiple virtual machines, AWS EC2 instances, and so on. The network load balancer will have logic to check if the downstream server is responding through ping checks or heartbeat or any other mechanisms and it will be considered whether it is to be eligible for distributing the traffic or not.

A layer 7 load balancer is used to distribute traffic to processes running on the virtual machines, EC2 instances, and so on. For example, a web proxy like HA Proxy or Nginx load balancing downstream web services behind it. It can also be a cluster of databases running behind a database load balancer.

When using the Layer 4 or Layer 7 load balancers to achieve resilience against datacenter failures, the VMs, EC2 instances, and so on, would need to be spread across datacenters or regions or maybe a different level where the spread is across different cloud providers.

The other option is an active/passive setup. In this case, necessary configuration changes are done to point to the different regions and the passive instances are made active.

There are different setups that can be done to achieve the resiliency of a datacenter or a cloud provider failure. Some of these setups will be costlier than the others. The level of availability that an organization wants to set up and maintain depends on two main factors:

- What is the risk appetite of failures?
- How much do they want to spend to go to the next level of availability in this less occurring failure scenario?

The advanced setup is where the infrastructure is spread across on-premise and cloud or multiple cloud providers with fallbacks in place to switch the traffic from on-premise to cloud or from one cloud provider to the other cloud provider.

Hardware

There can be hardware failures that can occur in the real world. Automatic failover to a new device or a new server can be done in a high availability setup for the hardware devices.

Link/ISP failover

Another type of failure that can occur is the link or the internet connection failure. When such an event occurs, a backup device will failover and traffic will be routed through the backup device. This is an active/passive setup where the backup or the secondary device will become active when the primary device fails.

Service

A service can go down due to a variety of reasons. By maintaining high availability by running multiple replicas of the service on virtual machines and load balancing using a layer 7 load balancer like HAProxy, Nginix, and so on, the incoming traffic can be serviced by other available instances.

Automated recovery can be set up to restart the service which went down. In these cases, the existing instances have to take the load temporarily until the service is recovered to bring it back to a running state.

In the case of PaaS platforms, like Kubernetes, the platform manages the number of replicas and we can enable auto-scaling wherever needed to create more instances based on the load. If there is no auto-scaling but minimum number of replicas are configured, Kubernetes will create a new instance if one of the instances goes down to maintain the same number of instances.

Database

Databases can be run as a cluster where the different nodes in the cluster replicate the data between themselves and are load balanced behind a load balancer. Also, database dumps can be taken at regular intervals to back up the data.

For example, in the case of MongoDB, multiple nodes can be run as a replica set. Replica set in MongoDB is where there are multiple nodes to achieve high availability and data redundancy. One of the nodes from the replica set gets elected as primary and confirms the write operations. The other nodes replicate data from the primary. When the primary node fails, one of the remaining nodes gets elected as a primary and promote themselves to be a primary.

One of the common problems in these primary-secondary setups is the split brain problem. When network connectivity breaks between primary and one of the secondaries, there is a risk that two nodes can assume that they are the primary as the secondary assumes primary is unavailable. If two nodes assume they are primary, they both start making changes to their local copies of data without replicating to the other node. This will lead to inconsistencies of data between the two nodes.

So the election mechanisms and node setup are carefully done to avoid the risk of a split brain.

For example, in the case of MongoDB, there is an option to use an arbiter node which does not replicate any data from primary and is used only for voting purposes. If there are only two nodes in a replica set and the network connectivity breaks between primary and secondary only, there is a risk of the secondary assuming it is the new primary now. By using the arbiter node, it will be able to communicate with primary and will avoid the secondary to get switched to become a primary.

Rate limiting/throttling

Rate limiting or throttling policies can be set up on APIs being accessed. Rate limiting policies restrict the number of requests that can be served by an API in a given time window.

On the other hand, throttling will queue requests when the set limit is crossed. Throttling can be useful in handling the spikes in traffic while not rejecting many requests.

As an example, the Resilience4j library can be used to achieve rate limiting.

Circuit breaker

A side-effect of the micro-service architecture is that a request goes through a number of services. For example, when there is a request from a user that passes through service A, to service B, to service C, and so on, and service C goes down or becomes faulty and returns errors to service B, the same will be sent back to service A. So all the services that are stacked up to the failing services will start receiving failures. This problem can amplify due to retry logics that are usually built-in, causing a larger traffic in the system than expected. To avoid these failures, cascading from one failure to other and impacting the system overall, circuit breaker can be used.

For example, Resilience4j and Netflix Hystric libraries can be used to achieve the circuit breaker pattern.

Handle retry storms

Retry logic between services can be handled as stated above, but there can be retries from users as well. For example, on a slow network, user may hit refresh multiple times. And there is another example where there might be some other issue in the system in of the services that causes slow responses or failure responses to users or its calling services. This may cause multiple users or services with in-built retry logic to retry and it can make things worse.

There are different approaches to this problem:

- **Limiting re-tries**: Limiting re-tries can be made as a fixed number or it can be implemented to control the number of retry requests as a percentage of the total number of requests in a given time.
- **Exponential back-off**: In this approach, there is an exponential delay between each retry attempt.
- **Jittering**: In this approach, a random delay is introduced between each re-try request.

A combination of approaches can also be used, such as adding a jitter to an exponential delay. The end goal is to both limit the retries and also to make sure that multiple retries across the system are not all happening at exactly the same time.

Conclusion

Chaos engineering can help uncover weaknesses in complex systems. It is to be performed to gain more knowledge on the system behavior through experiments.

Chaos engineering is often confused with stress testing or load testing. Testing is performed to verify if something is working as expected with known inputs or random inputs that are purposefully fed in, while chaos engineering refers to verifying system behavior with known failure conditions that were not traditionally part of any form of testing.

Also, chaos engineering is not a single solution for reliability and only one of the things that can be done to improve the reliability of an application.

In the next chapter, we will cover DevSecOps and AIOps.

Multiple choice questions

1. Chaos engineering as a practice was started by this company:
   a) Google
   b) Netflix
   c) Facebook
   d) Twitter

2. Chaos engineering is a part of the following form(s) of testing:
   a) Stress testing
   b) Load testing
   c) Functional testing
   d) None of the above

3. The following can be one of the failure that can be injected:
   a) Random process kill
   b) Network Latency
   c) HTTP failures
   d) All of the above

Answers

1. b
2. d
3. d

Chapter 11
DevSecOps and AIOps

As an organization matures in its site reliability engineering practices, it starts positioning itself into an ideal place where it can rapidly scale up its software service offerings. This creates many opportunities and opens up new avenues for the organization. In order to ensure that the potential of these opportunities is fully realized, it becomes imperative that the security practices of the organizations are able to keep up with the pace and scale of the software services and is embedded at all stages of the software build process and does not remain an afterthought.

To address this requirement of scaling up security measures and moving them towards the early part of the software release cycle, the practice of DevSecOps came into existence. DevSecOps focusses on the addition of security measures in the software build stages before the software hits the production environment and can prove to be very critical in the software service offering as it can eliminate potential security loopholes before the users start using the application.

Similarly, the performance, availability, and health of the applications required for a large-scale software practice can be continuously and proactively monitored, measured ,and improved only with the adoption of intelligent automation. AIOps has come into existence to help automate the IT operations which can help the teams to scale up their infrastructure and application support.

Structure

In this chapter, we will discuss the following topics:

- Understanding DevSecOps
- Introduction to AIOps
- Use cases with AIOps
- ChatOps example

Objective

Most large-scale software applications in today's world are distributed and can run on multiple platforms and multiple tech stacks. The advancement in the areas of automation and data analysis through technologies associated with machine learning and artificial intelligence has now opened up newer possibilities in the world of software development and sustenance, especially for large-scale software development factories.

In this chapter, the readers will learn about two advance concepts associated with building and managing large-scale software applications, DevSecOps and AIOps. The readers will be provided with practical examples to understand these topics better.

Understanding DevSecOps

As discussed in *Chapter 1*, the DevOps methodology ensures that the software release happens in a stable and consistent manner and is automated end to end. DevSecOps can be thought of as an extension to the build and release workflows to address the specific security during the software build and release process. As the name suggests, DevSecOps aims at breaking silos and brings the practices of software development, security, and operations together.

Gone are the days when managing security was the job of a single team often under the management of the **CISO (chief information security officer)**. The IT world has now evolved into a stage where security is considered the responsibility of all teams which have any sort of a role to play in the software development, build, release, and sustenance process. In short, security is now considered as everyone's responsibility.

DevSecOps builds up on this very mantra as it ensures that the security required during the pre-release cycle of software is dealt with appropriately and handled by the right team at the right time. In order to achieve this, all teams involved in the software development and release process, including the development team needs to understand their responsibility and should be skilled enough to execute it.

The three main responsibilities of the development teams related to security are:

- Code scanning for security
- Security issue tracking
- Resolving identified security issues

While issue tracking and resolving issues usually follow the standard processes within SDLC, code scanning is a practice which needs to be understood in detail as this is one of the newer practices that has been introduced by DevSecOps.

Code scanning for security

Since there are multiple hands involved during the development practice, merely depending on the developers to follow the best and secure coding practices is not sufficient. There is a possibility that vulnerabilities might have been introduced via code which can either put the user data at risk or perhaps provide hackers with the opportunity to target the application hosting environment. Some of the risks can also be introduced by external dependent software packages that are included in the final package that is built. Both of these vulnerabilities pose a high amount of risk and should be dealt with in a timely and appropriate fashion.

There are several code scanning tools available in the market today which help identify such gaps. Companies are embedding code scanning practices in their CI and CD workflows. Clearing these scans without any critical security findings is defined as a mandatory step before any code can get into production.

Automated code scans are always preferrable over manual reviews as they can scale faster, cover all areas of code and are less error prone compared to human driven code reviews.

The automated code scans or code analysis are of two types:

- **Static application security resting (SAST)**
- **Dynamic application security testing (DAST)**

Static application security testing

SAST, also known as white box testing or static code scan, is a security testing methodology that detects security vulnerabilities existing in the organization's software applications by analyzing source code before it is compiled or in a non-runtime environment. The static analysis of code will model the different control paths of the application and identify any security weakness present.

This will prevent vulnerabilities from affecting the application hosting environments as it provides the developers an opportunity to resolve the vulnerabilities in the pre-release stages. Static code complements DevOps perfectly as it enables an automated feedback loop. Any issues detected by these scans are sent back to the developers for remediation.

A limitation of static code analysis is that it cannot identify gaps in the business logic. Consider the following code snippet:

```
function getFullContactNumber(CountryCode) {
if (CountryCode == 91)
return "091-123-456-7899" // This is expected behavior
if (CountryCode == 51)
return "082-123-456-7899" // This is incorrect return value
}
```

In the above pseudo code example, static analysis will have no understanding of the fault in the code as there is nothing wrong with the way the code is written.

Dynamic application security testing

DAST is the method of identifying issues by examining an application while it is running. A static code analysis is usually more comprehensive in identifying security gaps as the dynamic test will only find security issues in pieces of code that are actually executed. But the dynamic analysis approach is able to find issues in more subtle areas which are not possible by the static analysis approach. These issues can be in the areas of any runtime events or for whichever values of variables the application behavior is deviating.

Dynamic analysis can be performed both in the production and pre-prod stages. Both approaches have their own merit and utility as they help identify any issues before they are faced by the user as well as helping in capturing the application behavior based on user interactions. When an application is in use, all kinds of data flows into the application which may have been missed in the simulated test data. While static code analysis treats both the same since it cannot see the data, dynamic code analysis will pick these up.

There are a number of tools for analyzing source code written in C++, C#, Java, Python, or other popular programming languages. Organizations can pick the tool(s) which fit them the best based on their DevOps pipelines as well as the current set of security toolset, programming languages in use, and so on.

Secure releases using Infrastructure as Code

Apart from development teams, the infrastructure team also plays a critical role in DevSecOps. A key responsibility of this team is the provisioning of infrastructure required for the development and release of the software. The infrastructure provisioning can be broadly divided between provisioning two types of infrastructure: production and non-production.

For the production usage, a more stable, higher capacity, and secure infrastructure is required. While traditionally the production environments were long lasting servers with frequent security and other OS patching in place, modern day applications are able to run on more dynamic environments like containers or immutable infrastructure which requires the images used for creation of the application servers to be patched rather than the servers themselves. These practices are enabled by integrating the application hosting environments with the DevSecOps (CI CD) pipelines which are capable of switching the existing infrastructure with new (more secure) infrastructure.

Non-production environments can again be categorized into two types. These are as follows:

- Development environment
- Test environment

The DevSecOps pipelines can be enhanced to ensure that both these categories of non-production environments are dynamic, secure in nature and are only made available when required. This can again be achieved by enhancing the CI CD workflows to turn of certain environments when not required or once their role in the release cycle is completed.

Introduction to AIOps

AIOps refers to the use of analytics and machine learning for improving IT operations functions. AIOps as a term was coined in 2016 by Gartner. As AIOps is about the use of analytics and machine learning. The base requirement for implementing AIOps is to have the required data.

In *Chapter 3: Introduction to SRE*, we have learned the responsibilities of SREs. The following are the lines from the given list of responsibilities that can be achieved by using the techniques under the AIOps umbrella:

- Setup a mechanism to co-relate incidents that are caused by a single root problem.
- Predict failures where possible even before they occur.
- Detect anomalies in service behavior.
- Capacity planning using forecasting algorithms to understand the future needs of the infrastructure.

The prior step for AIOps is to collect the required data through observability. Without sufficient data, AI will not be effective.

In order to build a machine learning model, data has to be collected or created. Data needs to be collected and made available in an easy manner by aggregating and providing the best visualization.

Chapter 7: IT Monitoring and *Chapter 8: Observability* mention collecting logs, metrics, and traces. In addition to this data, the following is the useful data for SREs to help in reducing **MTTI (mean time to insight)** and **MTTR (mean time to recover)**:

- **Data about releases of new changes**: The useful information at the minimum about a release is the version number and the time when the release is done.

- **Release impact guides**: The release impact guides include the functional areas that are being modified by a release. The release impact guides may not play a major role in an application built using micro-services where each micro-service handles a specific piece of functionality. However, it will play an important role in the case of monoliths. It will be useful for SREs to know which part of the application(s) is/are modified in the new release.

- **New major market/product/project launch dates**: When there are specific dates where new products are launched or projects go live, there is a possibility of a spike in traffic or a new type of data being processed by the services.

  It may appear that a new launch or going live might be tied to a release. But it is not always true. I have worked in certain applications where we put code flags and the flag will be enabled at a later stage for the functionality to be enabled. And this flag is sometimes enabled from an UI as opposed to a configuration change via a release. This was primarily used in my experience working in capital markets back office applications where changes have to be enabled along with the rest of the market participants. So new functionality can be switched on by a user from UI.

- **Promotional program dates/Festival/holiday dates**: On these specific days, there will be a spike in traffic. If there is any alert about increased volume, SREs can relate to the promotional program which is going on.

- **Infrastructure upgrades**: While there are releases to application, there are also changes done to the underlying infrastructure. This can be a move to a new infra which performs better or helps in any other areas. The upgrade can sometimes be a smaller one like an OS upgrade. In any case, this information will be useful.

- **Service connection topologies**: Connection topologies of which services are interacting with which other services will be useful.

- **Network topologies**: Network topology of how the infrastructure is set up and how different devices are connected is another piece of useful information.

Use cases with AIOps

Once the required data is available, many things can be achieved using AI. Some of these are mentioned in the next section.

Intelligent alerting

With available data, AI can be used to generate alerts based on detected anomalies. The anomaly can be with respect to the expected vs. the actual volume of traffic, the expected vs. the actual number of failures, and so on. There are a number of open source software tools available to perform forecasting using time series data.

Noise reduction

By co-relating the alerts, the alerts which have the same cause can be grouped together. For example, if there is an issue in an authentication service, multiple services that use the authentication service will be impacted. Any alerts about spikes in authentication failures across services can be all be grouped together into one main alert as the overall spike in the authentication failures. The others can be filtered out or the information in the alert can be enhanced as that an overall increase in authentication failures has been detected. SREs can then quickly know that there is a larger problem.

Automated root cause analysis

As data is available from different systems and different types of data mentioned above are available, this makes it possible to provide SREs with the potential root cause of the problem. By helping SREs narrow down the problem faster and by providing the data, the MTTI will reduce and further help in reducing MTTR.

In the above example of intelligent alerting, the alert can be enhanced with further data. For example, if the alerts originated minutes after a release was done to the login service, the alert can include information that there was a recent release in that service. With this insight, the SREs can then quickly check and take necessary remediation action.

Automated remediation

Automated remediation is the ability to automatically identify a problem and remediate with known remediation mechanisms. In the same example above, assume that there was an automated rollback mechanism in place. With the identified problem of a release update causing problems, the same can be identified and remediated with an automated rollback.

While mentioning these things of co-relation, automated analysis and intelligent alerting are easy in writing. In the real life, it will take effort to put the data together, train and build models, and set up the right workflow for an automated remediation as described above. Sometimes, there can be a need for a manual intervention between an automatically identified problem and a recovery. An SRE can verify and let the remediation to occur with pre-built steps.

StackStorm is an example of an open source software that can be used to set up automated remediation workflows.

ChatOps

ChatOps as a term existed even before AIOps and involves the use of machine learning in creating conversational agents with which the SREs can interact with. An example use case of ChatOps is to build a ChatBot for an SRE to instruct commands. For example, imagine a case where an SRE decides to restart a particular service. He/she can simply open a chat window with the bot and can say "Please restart XYZ service" and the bot will do the job for the SRE. We will see an example of a ChatBot that can understand these instructions later in the chapter by using the open source Rasa software.

As another example, a bot can be used to send messages to a Slack channel notifying about an incident.

ChatOps example with Rasa, Flask, and Telegram

There are multiple options in building chatbots and for the example in this book, we will use Rasa, Flask, and Telegram. Any chatbot that needs an ability to take an action by parsing and understanding the user entered text needs three main things. These are as follows

- A way to understand the intent of the user as to what the user is saying and a way to extract the specific fields from the text to take an action from the user input. Technically, it's about intent classification and **Named Entity Recognition** (**NER**). For this, we will use the open source Rasa, in particular, Rasa NLU.

- A user interface for user to input the text. For this, we will use Telegram which can be used to create bots as well.

- A backend service to receive the text, take the necessary action, and respond back. For this, we will use Flask.

First, we will create a bot in Telegram. A chatbot can be created in Telegram by interacting with the BotFather user id in Telegram. As an example in this book, we have created a bot called MongoSREBot. On requesting a new bot with the **/newbot** message to the BotFather, an HTTP API token will be provided. The message from BotFather will include the following text:

```
Use this token to access the HTTP API:
```

```
<API Token>
```

```
Keep your token secure and store it safely, it can be used
by anyone to control your bot.
```

Chatbot in Telegram can be integrated with a web application using webhooks (in simple terms, it will be POST requests). Whenever a message is sent to the chatbot in Telegram, a POST request is made to the registered endpoint.

We will create a web app using Flask which will have the POST end point to receive REST calls from Telegram.

The following are import lines from the Flask app which will register the webhook. <Some random hex> is a random hexadecimal value,

"API Token" is provided by the BotFather while creating the bot. And **domainname** is the domain on which the Flask app is running.

```
from flask import Flask, request
import telepot
secret = "<some random hex>"
bot = telepot.Bot('<API Token>')
bot.setWebhook("https://www.<domainname>.com/{}".format(secret), max_connections=1)
```

Then the Flask app needs to have a route to receive the calls from Telegram when the user sends a message to parse the text and send back the response. You can see the secret within the decorator.

After explaining about Rasa NLU, we will take a look at the code that can go inside **telegram_webhook**.

```
@app.route('/{}'.format(secret), methods=["POST"])
def telegram_webhook():
```

Next, we will setup Rasa NLU. For the purpose of the example in this book, we will use the Rasa NLU 0.12.2 version. Installation can be done using **pip** command.

```
pip install rasa-nlu==0.12.2
```

Rasa provides different options of the other modules that can be used for things like tokenization, NER, and intent classification which are part of processing for **Natural Language Understanding** (**NLU**). We will use spacy pipeline which uses spacy for tokenization, sklearn for intent classification, and **Conditional Random Fields** (**CRF**) for named entity recognition. Further details about NER and CRF are out of the scope of this book.

Spacy can be installed using the following commands. In this example, we are using the English language package. This can be set up with the following commands:

```
pip install --user https://github.com/explosion/spacy-models/releases/download/en_core_web_sm-2.0.0/en_core_web_sm-2.0.0.tar.gz
python -m spacy link en_core_web_sm en_default
```

In order to use the spacy pipeline, the following is the content in the config file which is needed for building the model:

`language: "en"`

`pipeline: "spacy_sklearn"`

We are using the supervised learning approach here where we will be using data to train and build the model to be used later for parsing the user text. The data in this case will be a JSON file. The following is a section from the JSON file which has the training data that tells that in the line "Please restart login service," "Login" is the name of the service, and the service by itself is a process. Login and service are the two entities that will be extracted from the user text when this text is input. The intent from the user is **restartService**. The full file can be found at the following:

https://github.com/xfgeek/mangosrebot.git.

```
{
        "text": "Please restart login service",
        "intent": "restartService",
        "entities": [
          {
            "start": 15,
            "end": 20,
            "value": "Login",
            "entity": "ServiceName"
          },
          {
            "start": 21,
            "end": 28,
            "value": "Service",
            "entity": "Process"
          }
        ]
      },
```

After building the training file, the next step is to build the model. The following is the command to build the model:

```
python -m rasa_nlu.train --config config_spacy.yml --data data/sreExample.json --path sreproject
```

The following is the output that is generated by the above command confirming that the training is complete. If there are any exceptions, the training process will fail and the relevant exception will be provided.

```
Fitting 2 folds for each of 6 candidates, totalling 12 fits
[Parallel(n_jobs=None)]: Done   12 out of  12 | elapsed:    0.0s finished
```

On running the **train** command, the model is built in the given path of **sreproject**.

```
20:40 ~/sreproject/default $ ls -ltr
total 4
drwxrwxr-x 2 myfd registered_users 4096 Dec 23 19:52 model_20201223-195238
20:40 ~/sreproject/default $ pwd
/home/myfd/sreproject/default
```

After the model is built, we will come back to the Flask app code and look at the full code inside the route created to receive the POST requests.

The first line is to receive the request data in THE JSON format.

```
@app.route('/{}'.format(secret), methods=["POST"])
def telegram_webhook():
    botInput    = request.get_json()
```

The next is to load the interpreter with the trained model.

```
    interpreter = Interpreter.load('/home/myfd/sreproject/default/model_20201223-195238/')
```

The next step is to extract info from the JSON and parse the user message.

```
    chatId      = botInput["message"]["chat"]["id"]
```

```
        text                    =
unicode(ignorenonascii(botInput["message"]["text"]), 'utf-
8')
        parsedData  = interpreter.parse(format(text))


        if 'first_name' in botInput["message"]["chat"]:
            userName = botInput["message"]["chat"]["first_
name"]
        else:
            userName = ''
```

If the user intent based on the intent classification by Rasa NLU is **restartService**, run the necessary command to restart the service. For this example, we will ignore the command. The command will vary based on where the service is deployed. A Similar logic can be kept for other intents.

```
        if parsedData['intent']['name'] == 'restartService':
            # Bot actual action
            botReply = "Service restarted successfully"


        if parsedData['intent']['name'] == 'greet':
            botReply = "Hi " + userName
```

The final step is to reply back to the user in Telegram.

```
        try:
            bot.sendMessage(chatId, botReply)
        except:
            print("Error responding to user")


        return "OK"
```

We can test by sending a test message to the bot.

DevSecOps and AIOps ▪ 199

> **Vishnu Vardhan Chikoti** — 1:36:27 AM
> Hi
>
> **MangoSREBot** — 1:36:39 AM
> Hi Vishnu Vardhan Chikoti
>
> **Vishnu Vardhan Chikoti** — 1:36:49 AM
> please restart login service
>
> **MangoSREBot** — 1:36:50 AM
> Service restarted successfully

Figure 11.1

You can extend the bots ability by adding more training data for various intents and logic inside the webhook for actions based on the intent and extracted entities.

Conclusion

While DevSecOps and AIOps are two different fields, in practice, often the boundaries between these can blur in certain areas. Both these practices are based on the foundation of automation and instrumentation of the environments which to some extent can be achieved through the DevSecOps pipelines which can complement AIOps by ensuring the required data for capturing and reacting to application and user behaviors that are made available for AIOps. It should be noted that it is important to walk before you run and for an organization to be able to implement the advanced capabilities of SRE like DevSecOps and AIOps, the foundation should be laid first.

In the next chapter, we will take a look at the culture of site reliability engineering.

Multiple choice questions

1. **DevSecOps as a practice is applicable in the following software environment(s):**
    a) Development environment
    b) Test (QA, UAT) environment

c) Production environment

d) All of the above

2. The following is the main requirement for achieving AIOps:

    a) Chat application

    b) Web application

    c) Relevant Data

    d) None of the above

3. The following is/are the use case(s) under AIOps:

    a) Intelligent Alerting

    b) Noise reduction

    c) Automated Remediation

    d) All of the above

4. Webhooks typically use the following method:

    a) GET

    b) POST

    c) PUT

    d) None of the above

Answers

1. d
2. c
3. d
4. b

CHAPTER 12
Culture of Site Reliability Engineering

As site reliability engineering is predominantly a practice applied in the area of technology, it is easy to focus only on the relevant technical areas and respect the technical knowledge of individuals over their people skills, mindset, and the cultural aspects associated with successfully implementing SRE.

Any number of tools and technologies will not be able to deliver the value of SRE unless there is a buy-in at all levels. A firm belief is required that SRE can drive a positive change in the organization and will play a critical role in the success of an advanced digital organization.

Structure

In this chapter, we will discuss the following topics:

- Breaking silos in the organization
- Embracing risk
- Continuous improvement

Objective

Along with driving a change in the technical practices and processes within the organization, there is a change required in the culture of the teams which puts the success of the team at the center and not on individual brilliance. This will ensure that the transformation towards SRE occurs at an organizational level and is not on the shoulders of a select few star performers.

A bold mindset along with a keen eye for improvements by all is a very important aspect that needs to be understood for the success of SRE. The focus in this chapter will be on the change required in the mindset of people and the prevalent culture of the organization.

Breaking silos in the organization

Since there is an inherent conflict between the development teams that are striving for agility, speed, and the operations team whose focus is to maintain stability, it is easy for these two teams to drift apart and not collaborate enough. Studies have indicated that majority of the costs of a software are incurred after it is launched and this needs to be acknowledged and addressed by these two teams involved in these critical stages.

Adding to these challenges are the expectations of the business teams who are driven to satisfy the external customers. Most of the decisions of the business teams are centred around the needs of the customers and seldom are efforts made to consider the internal factors which play a critical role in solution delivery.

This often leads to bottlenecks occurring at different areas, dissatisfaction within team members, and poor-quality solutions creeping into the environment. SRE addresses this challenge by a shared ownership model between these teams. The two key areas within SRE, **service level objectives (SLOs)** and error budgets which have been discussed in detail in the previous chapters, play a key role in breaking these silos. While determining the values for SLOs and error budgets, SRE ensures that team members across teams and at all levels are coming together to understand the needs of the business and the quality of service that can be delivered.

Common incentives are defined for SREs and the developments teams to meet the reliability goals and to achieve these, it becomes imperative that these teams are constantly collaborating and evolving together. Staying within the error budget and meeting the SLOs will ensure that the software can be delivered faster, all the while maintaining stability which satisfies the development teams as well as the operations teams.

Embracing risk

A key principle of SRE is to understand that the goal is not to make the system available 100% of the time. In any software service, there are factors other than the software reliability itself which also play a key role in the overall reliability of the service experienced by the users. These services can be network availability and the speed of the users, configuration of the client device, and so on. This means that it is not easy for users to distinguish between a service which has high reliability and a service which has very high reliability.

Once a certain level of reliability is achieved, it might make more business sense to invest in innovation and feature creation than striving towards even more high reliability. Digesting this fact seems a very difficult task but is a beginning step towards accepting what the truth is about any system. This is what is called as embracing risk in SRE.

When we accept that the system is bound to go down, we can move on to determining what the risk associated with a service going down is and the measures that can be taken to minimize this risk. Risk reduction means determining ways of measuring risk, managing risk, and eliminating risk.

Continuous improvement

As discussed earlier, there are a number of practices of SRE which need an understanding of the environment, the roles played by all teams and individuals involved, and using data analytics to drive reliability. With these in mind, it can be easy to get carried away and spend way too much time in getting everything exactly right. This is a pitfall that should be avoided.

While implementing SRE, it is important to get things started once a fair amount of due diligence is done. Nothing is set in concrete upfront, except for any legal contracts like SLAs with the customers for which a certain amount of buffer should be ensured while agreeing to the internal quality and service level metrics. Once these levels are set, then the metrics and baselines should be reviewed periodically and can be redefined if required.

As the software service is being used, enough instrumentation should be done in it to ensure that feedback to the respective teams, in terms of inputs around the usage of the service and the reliability of the service, keeps flowing in. Based on this feedback, the reliability improvements should be induced as and when necessary.

Intelligent automation

A scalable way of doing these improvements is by relying on automating the following:

- **Feedback/usage metrics aggregation**: It is important that the software services have built-in mechanisms like telemetry to help understand usage related metrics and performance measuring capability enabled by monitoring tools. The data generated from these systems should be directed towards a system which can aggregate it and analytics can be performed on this.
- **Feedback analysis**: By performing analytics on the data obtained from these different sources, useful insights like bottlenecks in the system, performance challenges, most used features, optimal capacity, and others can be obtained.
- **Automated improvements**: Once these insights are obtained, the next step should be towards determining the optimization process for the challenges identified. To ensure that these insights are driving improvements and can be scaled, it becomes imperative that these improvements are automated.

Shift-left mindset

Incorporating continuous improvements and automation into your software development and operations processes which results in uncovering bottlenecks earlier and less expensive to fix is considered as shift-left in SRE. The more that individuals in both development and operations teams can adopt this practice, the higher that reductions in the software development services can be achieved.

By constantly evaluating the quality of software and release, inducing quality improvement measures can become that much simpler and cost efficient as the effect on production services is reduced and business remains unimpacted.

Conclusion

Driving change in any complex business environment requires a proper change management program. The changes required to be adopted for successful implementation of site reliability engineering are no different. For SRE to be embedded as a day-to-day practice, the cultural aspects discussed in this chapter are equally important to be adopted.

Site reliability engineering as a software reliability practice is still in its early stages and is bound to evolve with time as more organizations adopt it and customize it for their respective teams. What will remain more or less the same is the progressive, blameless, and team-first mindset required for the success of this program.

Multiple choice questions

1. **A key principle of SRE is to understand that the goal is not to be ___ available.**
    a) 90%
    b) 95%
    c) 100%
    d) 99%

2. **Intelligent automation involves the following key step(s) to be followed:**
    a) Feedback aggregation
    b) Feedback analysis
    c) Automated improvements
    d) All of the above

Answers

1. c
2. d

Index

A
Active Directory (AD) 63
agents 110, 111
AIOps 190, 191
AIOps, use cases
  about 192
  automated remediation 193
  automated root
      cause analysis 192, 193
  ChatOps 193
  Intelligent alerting 192
  noise reduction 192
Ansible
  about 34
  inventory 34, 35
  modules 35
  playbooks 35-37
application monitoring
  about 105, 106
  database monitoring 108
  logs, checking 106, 107
  MQ monitoring 108
  probes 106
  processing
      time, capturing 107, 108
application teams, role
  about 11
  cross-functional development
      teams 11, 13
  DevOps teams 14, 15
  operations teams 15
  production support teams 15
automated testing 28

B
blameless
    postmortems 46, 88, 89
blue-green
    deployment 29, 74-81

C

Canary deployment 29, 81-83
Cardinality attributes 132
cf push command 10
chaos engineering
  about 163
  application/service
    unavailability 163, 164
  configuration errors 165
  database failures 165, 166
  network delays 164
  network failures 164, 165
  resource unavailability 165
chaos engineering process
  about 166
  automation 168
  blast radius, minimizing 167
  failure condition, injecting 167
  hypothesis, building 166
  hypothesis, verifying 167
  issues, fixing 168
  reverse failure condition 167
  steady state, defining 166
Chaos GameDay 168
ChatOps example
  with Flask 194-199
  with Rasa 194-199
  with Telegram 194-199
chief information security
    officer (CISO) 186
circuit breaker 181
command line
    interface (CLI) 107
Conditional Random
    Fields (CRF) 195
content delivery
    networks (CDNs) 45
continuous
    deployment (CD) 28
continuous integration and
    continuous deployment
    (CI/CD) tools 14

continuous
    integration (CI) 28, 72

D

data files 58
data transformation 111
deadlocks 109
development teams
  role 94-98
DevOps
  about 24, 25, 42, 43
  benefits 31
DevOps practices
  about 26, 27
  automated testing 28
  blue-green deployment 29
  canary deployment 29
  continuous deployment 28
  continuous integration 28
  immutable infrastructure 30
  Infrastructure
    as Code (IaC) 29, 30
  logging 30
  monitoring 30
  secrets management 31
  serverless computing 31
DevOps principles
  about 26
  automation 26
  collaboration 26
  continuous improvement 27
  security 27
DevOps tools
  Ansible 34
  Git 32, 33, 34
  Jenkins 37
  overview 32
DevSecOps
  about 186, 187
  code scanning,
    for security 187

Index — 209

secure releases, with
　Infrastructure as Code
　(IaC) 189, 190
DNS monitoring 110
Domain Name
　System (DNS) 18, 19
dynamic application security
　testing (DAST) 188, 189

E
ElastAlert
　reference link 122
Elastic Compute Cloud (EC2) 9
end to end monitoring
　strategy 102, 103
end user monitoring 109, 155
error budget
　about 46, 157, 158
　policy 158

F
failure injection 169
failure injection, commands
　HTTP failures 176-178
　multiple failures, injecting 178
　network failures 170, 171
　process killing 170
failure injection, tools
　ChaosBlade by Alibaba 169
　Chaos HTTP Proxy 170
　chaoskube 169
　ChaoSlingr 169
　Chaos Mesh 169
　Cthulhu 169
　Mangle by VMware 169
　Muxy 170
　Resiliency Studio
　　by AT&T 170
　Sitespeed.io Throttle 170
　Spring Boot Chaos
　　Monkey 169
Filebeat 133-136
File Transfer Protocol (FTP) 17
Flask
　using, in ChatOps
　　example 194-199
Fluentd
　about 142-145
　reference link 142
functional testing 14

G
Git 32-34
Google Cloud
　Platform (GCP) 10
Grafana 119

H
HTTP-Secure (HTTPS) 17
Hypertext Transfer
　Protocol (HTTP) 17

I
identity and access management
　(IAM) 62, 63
immutable infrastructure 30
incident
　about 86
　lifecycle 87
　properties 86
incident communication 92
incident example
　about 89
　incident communication 92
　incident
　　detection/notification 89
　incident resolution 93
　incident retrospective/
　　postmortem 94
　incident triage 90, 91
incident knowledge base 94
incident management 65-67, 86
incident priority
　levels 91, 92
incident resolution 93
incident retrospective 94

incident severity
  levels 91
Infrastructure as Code (IaC)
  about 29, 30
  using, for release
    management 73
infrastructure
    decommissioning 64, 65
infrastructure monitoring
  about 103
  network monitoring 104
  server monitoring 104
  storage monitoring 104, 105
infrastructure
    provisioning 64, 65
infrastructure teams, role
  about 7
  cloud infrastructure 9
  containerization 8
  data centers 7
  development and deployment
    platforms 10
  on-premise infrastructure 9
  virtualization 8
intelligent automation 204
internet companies 43, 44
Internet Protocol (IP) 17
IT function
  application development 4
  application hosting 4
  compliance and security 3
  core software services 3
  Enterprise Architecture (EA) 5
  hardware availability 3
  role 2
  software delivery 5
IT organization structure 6
IT security
  about 15, 16
  change management team 16

J
Jenkins 37
Jenkins, key concepts
  jobs 38
  slaves 39

K
Kubernetes 10

L
launch checklist 47
Linux 171, 172
logging 30
Logstash 137-140
long running queries 108

M
MacOS 172, 173
mean time between failures
    (MTBF) 47
mean time to detect
    (MTTD) 47, 94, 102, 129
mean time to investigate
    (MTTI) 129, 191
mean time to recover
    (MTTR) 47, 129, 191
mean time to resolve
    (MTTR) 94, 102
Metricbeat
  about 115-117
  download link 115
Microsoft Azure 10
Model-View-Controller
    (MVC) 12
monitoring 30
monitoring tools
  about 110
  agents 110, 111
  alerting 112
  collectors 111
  dashboarding 112
  data transformation 111
  ElastAlert 122-125

Grafana 119-122
Metricbeat 115-118
Prometheus 112-114
storage 112
transport 111
Muxy 174-176
MVC pattern
 components 12

N
Named Entity
  Recognition (NER) 194
Natural Language
  Understanding
  (NLU) 195
Netem 171, 172
Network Emulator (NetEm) 171
network monitoring 104
Network Operations
  Center (NOC) 102

O
observability
  Cardinality attributes 132
  pillars 130, 131
  standardized APIs 131
  standardized libraries 131
  standardized SDKs 131
  standardized trace context 132
  tracers 132
observability, goals
  about 128
  operational efficiency 129
  security and compliance 129
  service reliability 128
open source libraries and tools
  about 132
  Filebeat 133-136
  Fluentd 142-145
  Logstash 137-140
  OpenTelemetry 146-148
OpenTelemetry 146-148

P
packet filter (pf) 172, 173
performance and volume (P&V)
  testing 14
Pivotal Cloud
  Foundry (PCF) 10, 81
Platform as a Service (PaaS) 7
point-to-point protocol (PPP) 17
Potentially Shippable Product
  Increments (PSPI) 12
processed per second (TPS) 14
process optimization
  with automation 55, 56
production environment 15
project management
  office (PMO) 6
Prometheus 114
PythonAnywhere 10

R
Rasa
  using, in ChatOps
    example 194-199
rate limiting policies 181
rate throttling policies 181
RED method
  about 153
  duration 153
  errors 153
  rate 153
regression testing 14
release automation
  with CI/CD 72
release management
  about 70
  build package 71
  deployment 72
  Infrastructure as Code (IaC),
    using 73
  quality and security, testing 71
  release planning 71

resiliency techniques
  building 178
  circuit breaker 181
  rate limiting policies 181
  rate throttling policies 181
  retry storms, handling 182
  single point of failures 178
retry storms
  handling 182
retry storms, approaches
  exponential back-off 182
  jittering 182
  limiting re-tries 182
root server 18

S

secrets management 31
security information and event
    management (SIEM) 130
Security Operations
    Center (SOC) 102
serverless computing 31
server monitoring
  about 104
  key parameters 104
service level agreement (SLA)
  about 42, 156
  attributes 157
service level indicator
    (SLI) 45, 153-155
service level objective
    (SLO) 42, 45, 155, 156, 202
shift-left mindset 204, 205
single point of failures
  about 178
  database 180, 181
  datacenter 178, 179
  hardware failures 179
  link/ISP failover 179
  service 180

site reliability engineering (SRE)
  about 42, 43
  continuous
      improvement 203, 204
  key measurements 153
  key metrics 152
  overview 44
  risk, embracing 203
  silos, breaking in 202
  skill set 50, 51
  team responsibilities 49, 50
  terms 44, 48, 49
standardized APIs 131
standardized libraries 131
standardized SDKs 131
standardized trace context 132
static application security
      resting (SAST) 188
storage monitoring 104, 105

T

TCP/IP protocol suite 16
Telegram
  using, in ChatOps
      example 194-199
temporary files 59
testing types
  functional testing 14
  performance and volume
      (P&V) testing 14
  unit testing 13
time-to-live (TTL) 19
toil
  about 45, 54
  eliminating 55
toil example
  database tables, purging 59
  files, archiving 56, 57
  files, purging 56, 57
  identity and
      access management
      (IAM) 62, 63

incident management 65, 66
infrastructure
    decommissioning 64, 65
infrastructure
    provisioning 64, 65
installation 60, 61
log files, checking 62
monitoring 61
patching 60, 61
vulnerability
  scans 64
with automate approach 56
top level domain (TLD) 18
tracers 132
Traffic Controller (TC) 171
transaction log
  filling up 109
Transmission Control Protocol
    (TCP) 17

U
USE method
  about 153
  errors 153
  saturation 153
  utilization 153
user acceptance
    testing (UAT) 15
user datagram
    protocol (UDP) 17

V
vendor management
    office (VMO) 6
vulnerability scans 64

Printed in Great Britain
by Amazon